SUGAR BABIES
(The Burlesque Musical)

Conceived by
Ralph G. Allen and Harry Rigby
Sketches by
Ralph G. Allen
Music by
Jimmy McHugh
Lyrics by
Dorothy Fields   Al Dubin
Additional Music and Lyrics by
Arthur Malvin
Sugar Baby Bounce by
Jay Livingston and Ray Evans
Produced on Broadway by
Terry Allen Kramer and Harry Rigby

S A M U E L   F R E N C H ,   I N C.
45 West 25th Street   NEW YORK, N.Y. 10010
7623 Sunset Boulevard   HOLLYWOOD 90046
LONDON   *TORONTO*

Songs

ACT I:

Overture:

"A GOOD OLD BURLESQUE SHOW": (Music by Jimmy McHugh; Lyrics by Arthur Malvin) Copyright © 1979 by Jimmy McHugh Music Inc. and Arthur Malvin Music Co.

"LET ME BE YOUR SUGAR BABY": (Music & Lyrics by Arthur Malvin) Copyright © 1979 by Arthur Malvin Music Co.

"IN LOUISIANA": (Music by Jimmy McHugh; Lyrics by Arthur Malvin) Copyright © 1980 by Jimmy McHugh Music Inc. and Arthur Malvin Music Co.

"I FEEL A SONG COMIN' ON": (Music & Lyrics by Jimmy McHugh, Dorothy Fields, George Oppenheimer) Copyright © 1935 by Robbins Music Corporation, Copyright Renewed

"GOIN' BACK TO NEW ORLEANS": (Music & Lyrics by Arthur Malvin) Copyright © 1979 by Arthur Malvin Music Co.

"SALLY" (Music by Jimmy McHugh; Lyrics by Arthur Malvin) Copyright © 1980 by Jimmy McHugh Music Co. and Arthur Malvin Music Co.

"IMMIGRATION ROSE" (Music by Jimmy McHugh; Lyrics by Eugene West & Irwin Dash) Copyright © 1923 by Mills Music I Copyright Renewed

"DON'T BLAME ME": (Music by Jimmy McHugh; Lyrics by Dorothy Fields) Copyright © 1932 by Robbins Music Corporation; Copyright Renewed

"THE SUGAR BABY BOUNCE" (Music & Lyrics by Jay Livingston and Ray Evans) Copyright © 1979 by Jay Livingston and Ray Evans

"DOWN AT THE GAIETY BURLESQUE" (Music & Lyrics by Arthur Malvin) Copyright © 1979 by Arthur Malvin Music Co.

"MR. BANJO MAN": (Music & Lyrics by Arthur Malvin) Copyright © 1979 by Arthur Malvin Music Co.

"DON'T LISTEN TO THE SNOBS" Copyright © 1979 by Arthur Malvin Music Co.

Songs

ACT II:

"I'M KEEPING MYSELF AVAILABLE FOR YOU": (Music by Jimmy McHugh; Lyrics by Arthur Malvin) Copyright © 1980 by Jimmy McHugh Music Co. and Arthur Malvin Music Co.

"EXACTLY LIKE YOU": (Music by Jimmy McHugh; Lyrics by Dorothy Fields) Copyright © 1930 by Shapiro, Bernstein & Co., Inc.; Copyright Renewed

"WARM AND WILLING": (Music by Jimmy McHugh; Lyrics by Jay Livingston and Ray Evans) Copyright © 1959 by Twentieth Century Music Corporation

"CUBAN LOVE SONG": (Music by Jimmy McHugh & Herbert Stothart; Lyrics by Dorothy Fields) Copyright © 1931 by Metro Goldwyn Mayer Inc., Copyright Renewed

"EVERY WEEK ANOTHER TOWN" (Music & Lyrics by Arthur Malvin) Copyright © 1979 by Arthur Malvin Music Co.

"I CAN'T GIVE YOU ANYTHING BUT LOVE, BABY" (Music by Jimmy McHugh; Lyrics by Dorothy Fields) Copyright © 1928 by Mills Music Inc., Copyright Renewed

"I'M SHOOTING HIGH" (Music by Jimmy McHugh; Lyrics by Ted Koehler) Copyright © 1935 by Robbins Music Corporation, Copyright Renewed

"WHEN YOU AND I WERE YOUNG, MAGGIE BLUES": (Music by Jimmy McHugh; Lyrics by Jack Frost) Copyright © 1922 by Mills Music Inc., Copyright Renewed

"ON THE SUNNY SIDE OF THE STREET": (Music by Jimmy McHugh; Lyrics by Dorothy Fields) Copyright © 1930 by Shapiro, Bernstein & Co., Inc., Copyright Renewed

"YOU CAN'T BLAME YOUR UNCLE SAMMY": (Music by Jimmy McHugh; Lyrics by Al Dubin and Irwin Dash) Copyright © 1924 by Mills Music Inc., Copyright Renewed

"I WANT A GIRL (JUST LIKE THE GIRL THAT MARRIED DEAR OLD DAD) Copyright © 1911 by Harry Von Tilzer Music Publishing Company; Copyright Renewed (ᶜ/o THE WELK MUSIC GROUP)

"WHEN MY SUGAR WALKS DOWN THE STREET" (by Gene Austin, Jimmy McHugh and Irving Mills) Copyright © 1924 by Mills Music Inc., Copyright Renewed

Amateurs wishing to arrange for the production of SUGAR BABIES must make application to SAMUEL FRENCH, INC. at 45 West 25th Street, New York, N.Y. 10010, giving the following particulars:

(1) The name of the town and theatre or hall in which it is proposed to give the production.
(2) The maximum seating capacity of the theatre or hall.
(3) Scale of ticket prices.
(4) The number of performances it is intended to give, and the dates thereof.
(5) Indicate whether you will use an orchestration or simply a piano.

Upon receipt of these particulars SAMUEL FRENCH, INC., will quote the terms upon which permission for performances will be granted.

Stock royalties & foreign inquiries quoted on application to SAMUEL FRENCH, INC., 45 West 25th Street, New York, N.Y. 10010.

For all other rights than those stipulated above, apply c/o FITELSON, LASKY & ASLAN, 551 Fifth Ave., New York, N.Y. 10176.

A set of orchestral parts consisting of:

Piano Conductor Score
Pit Piano Score
Violin A
Violin B
Violin C
Cello
Reed I
Reed II
Reed III
Reed IV
Reed V
Trumpet I & II
Trumpet III
Trombone I
Trombone II
Trombone III
Percussion I # II
Bass
Harp
Horn

will be loaned two months prior to the production ONLY on receipt of the royalty quoted for all performances, the rental fee and a refundable deposit. The deposit will be refunded on the safe return to SAMUEL FRENCH, INC. of all loaned for the production.

Printed in U.S.A.

ISBN 0 573 68166 X

IMPORTANT ADVERTISING NOTE
BILLING

The names of the authors, lyricists, composers, and the original producers of the play must appear in all programs distributed in connection with performances, and in all instances in which the title of the play appears for the purpose of advertising, publicizing or otherwise exploiting the play and/or a production. The names of the authors, lyricists, composers, and producers must also appear on a separate line in which no other names appear, following the title of the play, and must appear in size of type not less than fifty per cent (50%) the size of the title type. The billing shall be in the following form:

(Name of Producer)
presents
(Names of Stars)
in
SUGAR BABIES
(The Burlesque Musical)
Conceived by
RALPH G. ALLEN and HARRY RIGBY
Sketches by
RALPH G. ALLEN
Music by
JIMMY McHUGH
Lyrics by
DOROTHY FIELDS   AL DUBIN
Additional Music and Lyrics by
ARTHUR MALVIN
"Sugar Baby Bounce" by
JAY LIVINGSTON and RAY EVANS
Produced on Broadway by
TERRY ALLEN KRAMER and HARRY RIGBY

MARK HELLINGER THEATRE

UNDER THE DIRECTION OF THE MESSRS. NEDERLANDER

TERRY ALLEN KRAMER AND HARRY RIGBY
in Association with COLUMBIA PICTURES
present

MICKEY ROONEY   ANN MILLER

in

SUGAR BABIES

The Burlesque Musical
Conceived by
RALPH G. ALLEN and HARRY RIGBY
Sketches by
RALPH G. ALLEN
Based on traditional material
Music by
JIMMY McHUGH
Lyrics by
DOROTHY FIELDS • AL DUBIN
Additional Music and Lyrics by
ARTHUR MALVIN
Sugar Baby Bounce by
JAY LIVINGSTON and RAY EVANS
Associate Producer
JACK SCHLISSEL
featuring

| SID STONE |

| JACK FLETCHER | BOB WILLIAMS | PETER LEEDS |
| JIMMY MATHEWS | SCOT STEWART | TOM BOYD |

and
ANN JILLIAN

Scenery and Costumes Designed by   *Lighting Designed by*
RAOUL PENE du BOIS   **GILBERT V. HEMSLEY, JR.**
Vocal Arrangements by
ARTHUR MALVIN
Additional Vocal Arrangements by
HUGH MARTIN and RALPH BLANE

Musical Director   *Orchestrations by*   *Dance Music Arranged by*
GLEN ROVEN   **DICK HYMAN**   **ARNOLD GROSS**
Associate Producers   *Hairstyles Designed by*
THOMAS WALTON ASSOCIATES   **JOSEPH DAL CORSO**
and FRANK MONTALVO

Entire Production Supervised by
ERNEST FLATT
Sketches Directed by
RUDY TRONTO

| *Staged and Choreographed by* |
| **ERNEST FLATT** |

CAST
(in order of appearance)

Mickey .... MICKEY ROONEY
Scot .... SCOT STEWART
Jillian .... ANN JILLIAN
Tom .... TOM BOYD
Peter .... PETER LEEDS
Jack .... JACK FLETCHER
Jimmy .... JIMMY MATHEWS
Ann .... ANN MILLER
Sid .... SID STONE

and
BOB WILLIAMS

THE SUGAR BABIES
LAURA BOOTH, CHRISTINE BUSINI, DIANE DUNCAN, CHRIS ELIA, DEBBIE GORNAY, BARBARA HANKS, JERI KANSAS, BARBARA MANDRA, ROBIN MANUS, FAYE FUJISAKI MAR, LINDA RAVINSKY, MICHELE ROGERS, ROSE SCUDDER, PATTI WATSON.
Alternates: LAURIE SLOAN, TERPSIE TOON.

THE GAIETY QUARTET
JONATHAN ARONSON, EDDIE PRUETT, MICHAEL RADIGAN, JEFF VEAZEY. Alternate: HANK BRUNJES.

UNDERSTUDIES
Understudies never substitute for listed players unless a specific announcement for the appearance is made at the time of the performance.
Ann Miller—Rose Scudder; Ann Jillian—Diane Duncan and Michele Rogers; Mickey Rooney, Jack Fletcher, Peter Leeds, Sid Stone, Jimmy Mathews—Tom Boyd; Scot Stewart—Michael Radigan; Tom Boyd—Hank Brunjes.

ACT I
1. **Overture**
2. **A Memory of Burlesque**
   Song: "A Good Old Burlesque Show" (Music by Jimmy McHugh;
   Lyrics by Arthur Malvin) .... Mickey Rooney and his friends
3. **Welcome to the Gaiety**
   Song: "Let Me Be Your Sugar Baby" (Music and Lyrics by Arthur Malvin)
   . . . Peter Leeds, Jack Fletcher and The Sugar Babies
4. **Meet Me 'Round the Corner*** .... Jimmy Mathews, Scot Stewart, Peter, Mickey, Rose Scudder, Chris Elia, Michele Rogers and Ann Jillian
   *One of the most famous of all Burlesque scenes, originally based on the Homestead Quartet, a minstrel show afterpiece.
5. **Travelin'**
   Songs: "In Louisiana" (Music by Jimmy McHugh, Lyrics by Arthur Malvin)
   "I Feel a Song Comin' On" (Music and Lyrics by Jimmy McHugh, Dorothy Fields,
   . . . George Oppenheimer)
   "Goin' Back to New Orleans" (Music and Lyrics by Arthur Malvin)
   . . . Ann Miller, The Sugar Babies and The Gaiety Quartet
6. **The Broken Arms Hotel** .... Jack, Tom Boyd, Mickey, Jimmy and Rose
7. **Feathered Fantasy (Salute to Sally Rand)** .... Scot, Barbara Hanks and The Sugar Babies
   Song: "Sally" (Music by Jimmy McHugh, Lyrics by Arthur Malvin)
8. **The Pitchman** .... Sid Stone
9. **Ellis Island Lament***
   Song: "Immigration Rose" (Music by Jimmy McHugh; Lyrics by Eugene West and
   Irwin Dash) .... Mickey and The Gaiety Quartet
   *Nearly all Columbia Wheel Burlesque Shows had quartets to support the principal comedian in his specialty turn. Among the more prominent examples are the Church City Boys in Louis Robey's **Knickerbockers** and The Four Harmonists in **The Girls from Happyland.**
10. **Scenes from Domestic Life** ....Jillian, Jimmy, Jack, Peter, Tom, Scott, Robin Manus, Laura Booth and Debbie Gornay

11. **Torch Song (After Bobby Clark)**
Song: "Don't Blame Me" (Music by Jimmy McHugh; Lyrics by Dorothy Fields)
. . . **Ann and Eddie Pruett**

12. **Orientale***
Christine Busini introduced by Jack
*Little Egypt, the sensation of the Columbian Exposition of 1893 and many imitators on the variety stages as did La Sylphe, a "Salome" dancer who caused a big stir in Burlesque in 1908.

13. **The Little Red Schoolhouse** .... **Ann, Rose, Diane Duncan, Jimmy and Mickey**

14. **The New Candy-Coated Craze***
Song: "The Sugar Baby Bounce" (Music and Lyrics by Jay Livingston and Ray Evans)
. . . **Jilian, Chris and Linda Ravinsky**
*There were many sister acts in Burlesque. The Watson Sisters owned their own company in the 1890's. The O'Connor Sisters were first featured in **Dave Marion's Own** show on the Columbia Wheel in 1923. Not many of the sister acts were comprised of actual sisters.

15. **Special Added Attraction: Madame Rentz and her All Female Minstrels***
featuring the Countess Francine
Introduction .... Jack
Songs: "Down at the Gaiety Burlesque" and "Mr. Banjo Man" (Music and Lyrics by Arthur Malvin) .... Ann, Mickey, Jeff Veazey and The Sugar Babies
*One of the earliest of all Burlesque Shows was the Rentz Troupe owned by M.B. Leavitt. Minstrel finales remained popular until 1925. Black light was used on the Variety stage as early as 1904, and there were no fewer than five black light numbers in **The Radium Girls of 1919.**

INTERMISSION

ACT II

1. **Candy Butcher** .... **Sid and The Gaiety Quartet**

2. **Girls and Garters***
Songs: "I'm Keeping Myself Available for You" (Music by Jimmy McHugh; Lyrics by Arthur Malvin)
"Exactly Like You" (Music by Jimmy McHugh; Lyrics by Dorothy Fields)
. . . **Jillian and The Sugar Babies**
*The first girl to throw garters at a Burlesque audience appears to have been Millie de Leon, "The Girls in Blue." Her act was a hot number on the circuits during the first decade of this century. As a result of her generosity, she spent several nights in jail.

3. **Justice Will Out** .... **Tom, Peter, Mickey and Ann**

4. **In A Greek Garden (Salute to Rosita Royce)**
Song: "Warm and Willing" (Music by Jimmy McHugh; Lyrics by Jay Livingston and Ray Evans) .... Jillian

5. **Presenting Madame Alla Gazaza** .... **Peter, Sid, Ann, Jeff, Mickey, Jimmy, Jack, Eddie, Jillian, Jonathan, Chris**

6. **Tropical Madness**
Song: "Cuban Love Song" (Music by Jimmy McHugh and Herbert Stothart; Lyrics by Dorothy Fields) .... Scot and Michele

7. **Cautionary Tales** .... **Rose, Jimmy, Eddie, Michael Radigan, Jeri Kansas, Jack, Peter, Tom and Sid**

8. **McHugh Medley** .... **Mickey and Ann**
Songs: "Every Day Another Tune" (Music and Lyrics by Arthur Malvin)
"I Can't Give You Anything But Love, Baby" (Lyrics by Dorothy Fields)
"I'm Shooting High" (Lyrics by Ted Koehler)
"When You And I Were Young, Maggie Blues" (Lyrics by Jack Frost)
"On The Sunny Side Of The Street" (Lyrics by Dorothy Fields)

9. **Presenting Bob Williams**

10. **Old Glory***
Song: "You Can't Blame Your Uncle Sammy" (Music by Jimmy McHugh; Lyrics by Al Dubin and Irwin Dash) .... The Full Company
*This finale commemorates a famous act, Madame Hilda Case and the Red Raven Cadets, who were headliners on the Empire Circuit in 1905.

Characters in the Scenes*

Mickey, first comic	*Mickey Rooney*
Scot, juvenile and singer	*Scot Stewart*
Jillian, soubrette	*Ann Jillian*
Tom, character man	*Tom Boyd*
Peter, straight man	*Peter Leeds*
Jack, character man	*Jack Fletcher*
Jimmy, second comic	*Jimmy Matthews*
Ann, prima donna	*Ann Miller*
Sid, eccentric comedian	*Sid Stone*

Also: various members of the male and female ensemble, including:

Chris	*Chris Elia*
Diane	*Diane Duncan*
Rose	*Rose Scudder*
Jeri	*Jeri Kansas*
Michele	*Michele Rogers*
Jonathan	*Jonathan Aronson*
Eddie	*Eddie Pruett*

*In Burlesque actors use their own given names to identify the characters they portray. The names in this script are the ones used in the original production of *Sugar Babies*. When other actors appear in the scenes, other names should be used.

Needless to say, producers should feel free to reassign the parts. Thus, for example, one actor need not play all the roles assigned to Mickey, if a different division of responsibilities would better suit the personalities of the cast and the circumstances of the production.

The notes and descriptions in this edition of the play are by Ralph G. Allen.

Sugar Babies

ACT ONE

SCENE 1

A MEMORY OF BURLESQUE

This number provides the pretext, however slight, for our light-hearted entertainment—a memory of Burlesque as seen through the eyes of the principal comedian of the show, who here acts as a presenter of a remembered or invented past. After the overture, the curtain parts to reveal, on a darkened stage, a roguish small FIGURE in silhouette, back to audience. The FIGURE is wearing a battered hat and a worn-out overcoat with brightly colored patches on the shoulders and elbows. A spotlight catches him. He turns and reveals himself to be the 1ST COMIC, a cheerful little man with an engaging smile. He acknowledges the audience and sings:

"A GOOD OLD BURLESQUE SHOW"

(ORCH: 4 Bar Intro)

1ST COMIC. (*Ad Lib*)
DON'T LISTEN TO THE SNOBS WHO SAY
BURLESQUE WAS MEAN AND LOW
BELIEVE ME THEY DON'T KNOW
THE HALF!
FOR A VERY MODEST PRICE
YOU COULD ENTER PARADISE
WHERE A MAN COULD DROWN HIS
TROUBLES IN A LAUGH
BOBBY CLARK AND LEON ERROL
WILLIE HOWARD, FANNY BRICE
AL JOLSON, SOPHIE TUCKER
EDDIE FOY
I REMEMBER EACH ROUTINE
ALL THE "SCHTICK"

IN ALL THEIR SCENES
IT'S A MEM'RY TIME CANNOT DESTROY
THERE WERE CHORUS GIRLS
AND JUGGLERS
AND A SENTIMENTAL TUNE
ILLUSTRATED BY A LANTERN SLIDE
NO FUN WAS EVER GREATER
THAT WAS *REAL* "THE-AY-TER"
I'D PAY A FIN TO BE INSIDE

(As the 1ST COMIC describes the glories of the vanished world which we are about to enter, that world comes alive for us.

A number of complex effects occur simultaneously. As the 1ST COMIC begins the second strain ("I would be happy . . ."), the lights come up to reveal the rest of the CAST posed as in a living picture from some old variety show. They are dressed as the stock characters of twenties' Burlesque. There are comic COPS and TOOTSIES and a voluptuous NURSE. There are ACROBATS and CON-MEN and HOOCHY-KOOCHY GIRLS. There are BUBBLE DANCERS and CANDY BUTCHERS and perhaps other familiar types as well. The choreographer may invent freely, drawing, like the author, on the memories of his misspent youth.

When the 1ST COMIC comes to the last line of the second strain ("I'd do a Burlesque show . . ."), the living pictures explode into action, and a comic ballet-pantomime ensues, during which the CAST performs many visual gags of ancient memory — an anthology, if you will, of the classic lazzi of Burlesque.

There are many bits to choose from, of course, and the choreographer again has wide latitude. However, he should make certain that the 1ST COMIC is the focal point of all the action. It is he who should get seltzer in his pants, have his pocket picked, suffer the indignity of a giant hypodermic in his bottom and otherwise be buffeted by the cruel tricks which a comic and malicious Fate has prepared for him. His misfortunes, however, must never seem to depress him. The 1ST COMIC of a Burlesque show never learns from his disappointment. He is a resilient creature, always hopeful, always eager for sex and the next adventure.

During the course of the ballet-pantomime, his worn overcoat is stripped from him, and he appears in one of the standard

*costumes of a top banana, perhaps baggy pants over cheer-
ful red underwear.*

*Also during the pantomime the stage itself is transformed from
a mean, shabby platform into a glorified version of a Burlesque house of the twenties.*

*The designer may make this transformation as simple or as
complex as time and resources permit. For example, it could
take place in three steps:*

*1. In this scheme, the first part of the song, including the living
picture effect, is played against a drop, possibly a scrim but
not necessarily so. The drop can be a simple neutral color or
it might be painted more elaborately. Perhaps it is a styliza-
tion of the empty stagehouse of an old theatre or a montage
of bits and pieces from the period background of Burlesque.*

*2. As the ballet-pantomime begins, the drop is raised or the
scrim bleeds through to reveal another drop on which a
display of Burlesque posters can be seen—advertisements
for the famous and obscure. "Madame Hilda and the Red
Raven Cadets;" "Bert Lahr in Blutch Cooper's Revue;" "The
Moonlight Maids, starring Billy Hagen;" "Billy Watson's
Beef Trust;" "Harry Gallagher in 'The Speed Girls of 1919';"
"Madame Rentz and her All-Female Minstrel Show."*

*3. Near the end of the song we become aware of a gaily-decorated
false proscenium just inside the real one. Perhaps it has
chaser lights. In any case the words "Gaiety Theatre" appear
on it somewhere. This false proscenium may be flown in
near the end of the song or permanently anchored and re-
vealed through a change of lights.*

*The three-step change need not be as lavish as the one I just de-
scribed. As in Burlesque itself, the audience can be invited
to piece out from imperfections with its thoughts. But,
however achieved, the number needs visual excitement—a
sudden transformation from dull neutral tones to vivid color,
from a soft glow to a blaze of light.*

*As the 1ST COMIC and the CAST sing the last note of the song,
an advertising drop descends in front of them, and the audience finds itself in the Gaiety Theatre of any town on the
circuit from Boston to Des Moines.*

There is no pause. The show-within-a-show begins.)

(ORCH: 4 Bars of a slow Soft-Shoe Feel)

1ST COMIC. (*continued, spoken, ad lib*) Red Skelton, Jim Bar-

ton, Phil Silvers, W.C. Fields . . . they all got their start in
Burlesque!

(*ORCH: Chorus*)

I WOULD BE HAPPY IF I COULD ONLY SEE
A GOOD OLD BURLESQUE SHOW
WITH ALL THE PERFORMERS
THE WAY THEY USED TO BE
IN A GOOD OLD BURLESQUE SHOW
TOP BANANAS WHO COULD
REALLY MAKE YOU SCREAM
AND THE KIND OF GIRLS
YOU PICTURE IN A DREAM
YA KNOW WHAT I'D DO
AND I'D DO IT ALL FOR FREE
A GOOD OLD BURLESQUE SHOW

(*ORCH: Tempo change to a Bright "Show 2" for the Pantomime
    Crossovers.*)

   1st COMIC & MEN.
HEY! WE'VE GOT A NUTTY GANG
AND WE CAN DO
A GOOD OLD BURLESQUE SHOW
YOU'RE GONNA SEE
BEFORE THE EV'NING'S THROUGH
A GOOD OLD BURLESQUE SHOW
GOT THE LADIES
AND THEY'RE GONNA MAKE YA SMILE

(*ORCH: Fill*)

WHERE'S THE GUY WHO SELLS
THE CANDY IN THE AISLE

(*ORCH: Fill*)

   CHARACTER MAN. (*shouting*) I'm here!!
   1st COMIC & MEN.
NOW WE'RE GONNA INTRODUCE YOU TO . . .
A GOOD OLD
BUR-
LESQUE
SHOW

ACT ONE

Scene 2

WELCOME TO THE GAIETY

The advertising curtain contains messages that recall the period: "Make the Gaiety a Weekly Habit;" "Liberty Bell Bail Bond Co.—Let Freedom Ring;" "Manny's Luncheonette—Where the Stars Eat." Enter STRAIGHT MAN. He is dressed in a tuxedo. A spotlight catches him by the right proscenium.*

STRAIGHT. Ladies and Gentlemen, before the start of tonight's performance, let me inform you about the policy of this theatre. There will be matinee and evening performances seven nights a week and a change of bill at the midnight show on Sunday. (*a chord from the ORCHESTRA*) Every Tuesday night is Garter Night. Every lady accompanied by a husband, whether hers or not, will receive absolutely free an intimate article of wearing apparel. (*chord*) Every Wednesday is Chorus Girl Opportunity Night . . .

(*Enter CHARACTER MAN. He is dressed in a suit, neat but ill-fitting. He stands at L. proscenium and with fierce concentration forces STRAIGHT to pay attention to him.*)

CHARACTER. Uh . . . uh . . . Peter.
STRAIGHT. Yes, Jack.
CHARACTER. I thought the folks out front would like to know that Miss Rosie Boots has been released on bail.
STRAIGHT. That's good to hear. (*Perhaps he starts some applause.*)
CHARACTER. She went a little too far at the Show Girl Opportunity Night, and the police took her in. She was supposed to rejoin the show tonight, but she couldn't make it.
STRAIGHT. Why not?
CHARACTER. Well, she was doing so well at the police station that they decided to hold her over for two more nights. (*exit, with a fixed stare at the audience*)

---

*NOTE: Real ads can supplement these fictional ones. Indeed an enterprising producer can make some extra money by selling space on the curtain to local firms who were in business in 1920.

STRAIGHT. (*resuming his announcement*) As I said, Wednesday night is Chorus Girl Opportunity Night. All chorus girls will compete for your applause with a dance of their choice. And coming soon . . .

CHARACTER. (*entering as before*) Just a minute, Peter. The management has asked me to make a special announcement.

STRAIGHT. Go right ahead, Jack.

CHARACTER. Starting next Thursday and every Thursday thereafter is Mothers' Night. So all you ladies who want to be mothers should meet the manager in his office after the show. (*exit as before*)

STRAIGHT. And coming soon . . . another big evening of Ladies' Boxing. And now . . . (*a drum roll*) Here they are, the ones that you've been waiting for, those tempting toe-tappers, smoother than honey and twice as sweet. Every girl a star in her own right—The Broadway Sugar Babies.

(*The ORCHESTRA plays a fanfare, the advertising drop rises, a traveller parts, and we begin the first musical number of the show-within-a-show.*)

ACT ONE

SCENE 3

EVERY GIRL A STAR

The CHORUS is introduced in a naive, vulgar, cheerful number that is typical of Mutual Burlesque.

As the traveller opens and the ORCHESTRA plays a 12-bar introduction, we see the SUGAR BABIES posed provocatively in front of a pink and blue drop. They wear boots, net stockings, feathered hats, handsome Gibson Girl bodices. While the ORCHESTRA vamps, they introduce themselves, shouting their names over the music: "I'm Diane!," "I'm Laura" . . . and so forth. They then come forward, form a traditional chorus line and sing a song of invitation to the audience.

"LET ME BE YOUR SUGAR BABY"
(*ORCH: Travellers open to 12 Bars in 3/4 and 1 Bar Intro into*)

DIANE. I'm Diane!
LAURA. I'm Laura!
ROBIN. I'm Robin!
BARBARA HANKS. I'm Barbara!
BARBARA MANDRA. I'm Bobbie!
CHRIS. I'm Chris!
ROSE. I'm Rose!
CHRISTINE. I'm Christine!
DEBBIE. I'm Debbie!
LINDA. I'm Linda!
JERI. I'm Jeri!
MICHELE. I'm Michele!
PATTI. I'm Patti!
FAYE. I'm Faye!

(*ORCH:*)

ALL GIRLS.
IF YOU'RE FEELING LOW
AND YOU JUST DON'T KNOW
WHY YOU'VE LOST YOUR APPETITE
HERE'S A REMEDY
THAT I GUARANTEE
SOON WILL HAVE YOU FEELING RIGHT

(*ORCH: 4 Bars to Chorus*)

LET ME BE YOUR SUGAR BABY
YOUR OWN CONFECTION
YOUR LOLLIPOP!
LET ME BE YOUR SUGAR BABY
YOUR YUMMY SUNDAE
WITH FUDGE ON TOP!

LET ME BE YOUR DANISH PASTRY

SOLO.
YOUR STRUDEL
SOLO.
YOUR CREPE SUZETTE
ALL.
HEAD TO TOE I'M A TREAT

AND YOU'LL FIND I'M
THE *SWEET*-EST SUGAR BABY
YOU'VE MET!

(*ORCH: 20 Bar Dance Section*)

   Girls.
LET ME BE YOUR SUGAR BABY
YOUR APPLE ASPIC
SERVED A LA CARTE
LET ME BE YOUR SUGAR BABY
YOUR UPSIDE-DOWN CAKE
YOUR PUMPKIN TART

YOUR PUDDING
MADE OF MOL — *ASSES*
YOUR DUMPLING
YOUR HONEYBEE
TAKE ME HOME TO YOUR MOTHER
YOU WON'T FIND ANOTHER
SUGAR BABY
BABY
BABY
LIKE
ME

(*ORCH: 12 Bar Exit*)
(*The song has a verse, a chorus, a 20-bar dance section and a
   reprise of the chorus. High spirits and high kicks predomi-
   nate. Finally there is a 12-bar exit in which the GIRLS form
   a chain and wave their goodbyes to the audience.*)

BLACKOUT

ACT ONE

SCENE 4

MEET ME 'ROUND THE CORNER

*After blackout, ORCHESTRA plays a signature tune; lights
   up on street scene in one. 2ND COMIC enters right,
   JUVENILE enters Left. They meet, ad lib greetings c.s.*

JUVENILE. Well, Jimmy.

2ND COMIC. Well, Scot.

JUVENILE. What have you been doing these days?

2ND COMIC. I've been working as a pilot in a livery stable.

JUVENILE. A pilot in a livery stable?

2ND COMIC. Yeh. I pile it here. I pile it there.

JUVENILE. Well, you sound as if you could use some money. You'd better join our quartet.

(*STRAIGHT enters right.*)

STRAIGHT. Hi, boys. Is this where the quartet is going to rehearse?

JUVENILE. That's right. But there's only three of us.

STRAIGHT. (*gesturing toward left proscenium*) Well, don't worry, boys. I've asked a friend of mine to join us, a man of culture and refinement. And here he comes now.

(*Enter 1ST COMIC in black pants and jacket. A dickey and black tie only partially conceal his red underwear. He is very disheveled and looks as if he has been thrown on the stage.*)

1ST COMIC. (*to wings*) I still don't think it was worth five dollars.

JUVENILE. Hi, Mick. It's good to see you. What have you been doing these days?

1ST COMIC. I've been working at a ladies' bloomer factory.

JUVENILE. Is it a good job?

1ST COMIC. Yeah, I pull down fifty a week.

STRAIGHT. Well, Mick, they need a quartet down at the Gaiety Theatre. Can you sing?

1ST COMIC. Sure. I used to sing in a queer.

STRAIGHT. No, no. You mean a choir.

1ST COMIC. It was a queer choir.

STRAIGHT. A queer choir?

1ST COMIC. Yes. We weren't even sure about the man who played the organ.

STRAIGHT. What do you mean?

1ST COMIC. He played nothing but hymns.

---

*Can be omitted in performance.

STRAIGHT. What was your best performance?

1ST COMIC. That would be the night I took the five cheerleaders to Atlantic City.

STRAIGHT. No, no, no. What was your best singing performance?

1ST COMIC. Oh, I used to sing in the opera. (*He begins to sing an aria.*)

STRAIGHT. What opera is that?

1ST COMIC. Madame Caterpillar.

STRAIGHT. No, you mean Madame Butterfly.

1ST COMIC. Well, I knew her before she was out of the cocoon.

STRAIGHT. Come on, boys. We'd better rehearse. What song shall we sing?

2ND COMIC. How about that old sailors' song?

STRAIGHT. What song is that?

2ND COMIC. "She Was Only a Fisherman's Daughter, But When I Showed Her My Rod, She Reeled."

STRAIGHT. I've got a better idea. We'll sing out of these books. (*He passes out songbooks.*) But first, we have to have a name for the quartet.

JUVENILE. How about the Avon Comedy Four?

STRAIGHT. Aw, no. That's too old-fashioned. We need something mellifluous. Something that will make the audience think of gentle zephyrs wafting over fields of new-mown hay. Something with an air about it.

2ND COMIC. How about the Shedhouse Quartet?

1ST COMIC. It does have an air about it.

JUVENILE. What page are we gonna sing on?

STRAIGHT. Sing on page fourteen.

2ND COMIC. There's no page fourteen in my book.

1ST COMIC. Sing on page seven twice. (*2ND COMIC sings a few bars of an aria. He hits 2ND COMIC with his songbook.*) Just a minute. What are you singing?

2ND COMIC. Paganini.

1ST COMIC. Whattya mean, Paganini? Let me see that.

2ND COMIC. See, it says right there, Paganini. (*shows 1ST COMIC the book*)

1ST COMIC. Paganini. You idiot. That says page nine.

STRAIGHT. Well, we've got to sing something. Have you any suggestions, Jimmy?

2ND COMIC. "I Want a Girl."

1ST COMIC. Let's sing first.

2ND COMIC. No. "I Want a Girl."

1ST COMIC. We don't want to know your personal problems.

JUVENILE. I think he means, "I Want a Girl Just Like the Girl That Married Dear Old Dad."

STRAIGHT. That's it. That's good.

1ST COMIC. Ladies and Gentlemen, you will now be entertained by the Shedhouse Quartet. (*He winces at the name. A triangle sounds, giving them the note. They sing, accompanied by the ORCHESTRA.*)

ALL.
I WANT A GIRL
JUST LIKE THE GIRL
THAT MARRIED DEAR OLD DAD
SHE WAS A PEARL
AND THE ONLY GIRL . . .

(*On "She was a pearl . . ." the 1ST GIRL enters. She is dressed like a tart. She walks, backed by the DRUMMER to the R. proscenium. As she passes SCOT, she drops her purse at his feet. While waiting for him to pick up the purse, she stands motionless except for some agitation of the hips. The MEN, of course, trail off in their song.*)

JUVENILE. Wait a minute, boys. That lady dropped her pocketbook, and me, being a southern gentleman, I shall pick it up and return it to her. (*He does so.*) Pardon me, lady, you dropped your pocketbook.

1ST GIRL. Oh, thank you. (*She opens the purse, then shuts it fast.*) And I can see that all my money is still there. Well, just for that, honey, you can . . .
MEET ME ROUND THE CORNER
IN A HALF AN HOUR;
MEET ME ROUND THE CORNER
IN A HALF AN HOUR;
MEET ME ROUND THE CORNER
IN—A—HALF—AN—HOUR.

(*During this recitation, she does a jazzy box step with a pelvic thrust, grinding on the last line and bumping on the last word. A follow spot narrows on her pelvis. When she bumps, the spot leaves her pelvis, arches across the street drop and goes out at left proscenium. Appropriate percus-*

sion accompanies this movement of light. 1ST COMIC starts to howl lustfully. He sounds as if he is in pain.)

STRAIGHT. Did she thrill you, Mick?

1ST COMIC. No. I just got my suspenders caught in my jockey shorts.

JUVENILE. (*at right proscenium, turns to OTHER THREE*) Boys, did you see what she said?

1ST COMIC. (*pointing at CLARINET PLAYER*) No, I was watching that guy wet his reed.

JUVENILE. (*same business as 1ST GIRL*) She . . . said . . . that . . . I . . . could . . .
MEET HER ROUND THE CORNER
IN A HALF AN HOUR;
MEET HER ROUND THE CORNER
IN A HALF AN HOUR;
MEET HER ROUND THE CORNER
IN . . . A . . . HALF . . . AN . . . HOUR.

(*JUVENILE grinds, bumps, exits. Spotlight hits 2ND COMIC. He reacts.*)

2ND COMIC. (*after brief pause, starts right*) I think I'll take him.

STRAIGHT. No, you don't, Jimmy. (*STRAIGHT grabs 2ND COMIC by the seat of his pants.*)

2ND COMIC. Hey, you're choking me.

1ST COMIC. Ladies and Gentlemen, you will now be entertained by the Shedhouse Trio. (*HE winces. The triangle again. ALL sing as before. On the same cue (i.e., "She was a pearl") 2ND GIRL enters, repeats the earlier business, only this time SHE drops a pocketbook with a brick in it. It hits 2ND COMIC's foot. HE yelps and pushes it to STRAIGHT.*)

STRAIGHT. That lady dropped her pocketbook.

2ND COMIC. She must have had a busy night.

STRAIGHT. Well, me being a southern gentleman, I will pick it up and return it to her. (*He does so.*) Pardon me, miss, you dropped your pocketbook.

2ND GIRL. Thank you, sir, and I can see that all my money is still there. Just for that you can . . .
MEET ME ROUND THE CORNER, etc.

(*Repeated three times as before, leading to grind, bump and
    exit. As she grinds, STRAIGHT crouches like a catcher.
    The spot leaves her pelvis. He catches it, throws it in the air.
    The spot circles around the auditorium as the COMEDI—
    ANS run around like outfielders under a pop fly. Finally,
    2ND COMIC catches it in his baggy pants.*)

2ND COMIC. (*with a big smile*) I got it.
1ST COMIC. That's all right. It'll be safe there.
STRAIGHT. (*now at left proscenium*) Hey, boys, did you see
what she said?
1ST COMIC. (*pointing at DRUMMER*) No, I was watching
that guy play with his tom-tom.
2ND COMIC. What did she say?
STRAIGHT.   Well,   she . . . said . . . that . . . I . . . could
MEET HER ROUND THE CORNER, etc.

(*Same business as before. On bump he hurts his back and limps
    off.*)

2ND COMIC. (*wiping his eye*) Hey, call your shots, will you.
1ST COMIC. Ladies and Gentlemen, you will now be entertained by the Shedhouse Brothers. (*He winces again. The
triangle sounds. Both sing. On "She was a pearl," 3RD GIRL
enters. Same business as before. She drops pocketbook in front
of 2ND COMIC, then waits at right proscenium.*)
2ND COMIC. That lady dropped her pocketbook. Maybe she'll
give us a reward.
1ST COMIC. Let's get the money first. (*Elaborate business here.
They look in purse, find no money. They dig in with more
determination. We hear a small accidental tear. A sheepish ex-
change of looks between them and a furtive glance at the GIRL
who hasn't heard anything and is not looking at them. 2ND
COMIC ad libs, "Damn, her motor's running," "She must be on
relief," etc. Now they shrug and rip it deliberately.*)
2ND COMIC. Oh, oh . . . (*The purse is torn to shreds. 1ST
COMIC holds it by a thread.*)
1ST COMIC. Give it back to her.
2ND COMIC. (*sheepishly*) This is going to be as noticeable as
hell. (*He presents her with the purse. She seems not to notice
the damage.*) Pardon me, miss, you dropped your pocketbook.
3RD GIRL. Thank you, and I see all my money is still there.

(*BOTH COMICS look startled.*)
    1st Comic. It should be. We couldn't find it.
    3rd Girl. Just . . . for . . . that . . . you . . . can . . .
MEET ME ROUND THE CORNER, etc.

(*She bumps and exits. Spotlight from her pelvis knocks off
    2ND COMIC's hat. The hat flies into 1ST COMIC's hands.*)

    1st Comic. I got it right here in the hat. (*He hands the hat to
2ND COMIC who looks into it thoughtfully.*)
    2nd Comic. If that don't grow hair, nothing will. (*He puts the
hat on.*) Hey, Mick, did you see what she said. She . . . said
. . . that . . . I . . . could . . .
MEET HER ROUND THE CORNER, etc.

(*As before, but 2ND COMIC is more enthusiastic than the
    OTHER MEN. 1ST COMIC gets ready to catch spotlight,
    ad libbing remarks like, "Put her here, boy," "Atta boy,
    Jimmy." When 2ND COMIC gets to third repetition and we
    expect him to end with a bump, he refuses to stop and does
    a fourth "MEET ME ROUND THE CORNER." The
    DRUMMER picks up the tempo. 1ST COMIC runs him
    off.*)

    1st Comic. (*alone*) You will now be entertained by Mr.
Shedhouse himself.
I WANT A GIRL
JUST LIKE THE GIRL
THAT MARRIED DEAR OLD DAD.
SHE WAS A PEARL . . .

(*No GIRL appears. 1ST COMIC sneaks a look at the wings
    and starts over.*)

    1st Comic. (*continued*) Must have run out of girls.
I WANT A GIRL
JUST LIKE THE GIRL . . .

(*still no GIRL*)

    1st Comic. (*continued*) Looks like I gotta change my tune.
(*He sings again.*)
MONEY, MONEY
MONEY GETS THE HONEY ALL THE TIME.

(*4TH GIRL enters hastily, adjusting her dress as if nervous about missing cue. She throws her pocketbook down like the other three GIRLS. 1ST COMIC picks it up. He is impatient with her.*)

1ST COMIC. (*continued*) Pardon me, miss, you dropped your pocketbook, and me bein' a southern-fried chicken, I'm goin' to return it to you. (*He hands it to her.*)

4TH GIRL. Thank you, and I see all my money is still there. And just for that . . . you . . . can . . . (*DRUMMER starts.*)
MEET ME ROUND THE CORNER
IN A HALF . . .

1ST COMIC. Wait a minute, honey. (*DRUMMER and GIRL stop. 1ST COMIC beckons to her. She joins him* c.s.) There were three girls out here. They all said:
MEET ME ROUND THE CORNER
IN A HALF AN HOUR . . .

(*does a little grind*)

1ST COMIC. (*continued*) My three friends were weak. They went round the corner. (*very tough*) But I don't go round no corners. Anything you want to do or say to me, you can do right here.

4TH GIRL. (*rubs his stomach*) Oh, please . . .

1ST COMIC. (*wilting a bit*) No, I don't go round no corners.

4TH GIRL. Oh, won't you please come around the corner?

1ST COMIC. (*weak with excitement*) Lady . . .

4TH GIRL. Yes?

1ST COMIC. Won't you please make bigger circles? (*She does so.*) A little lower and to the left. (*She continues to rub his stomach. He is very excited now. She is making wrinkles in his shirtfront.*) Look, you've taken the starch out of my dickey.

4TH GIRL. I can't stand it. I'm going to kiss ya, kiss ya, kiss ya. (*She does. A pop from the DRUMMER when they break apart.*) Oh, honey, honey . . .

1ST COMIC. Yes?

4TH GIRL. Now how do you feel?

1ST COMIC. Oh, I feel alright. But that guy out there . . . (*pointing at first row*) . . . is sweating like hell.

BLACKOUT

      SUGAR BABIES

ACT ONE

Scene 5

TRAVELIN'

In Burlesque and related entertainments, there was no more popular theme for a musical number than taking a trip—especially by train. The usual destination was in the South. Trains on the variety stage often went to Chattanooga, Alabam' or New Orleans, but almost never to Rochester or Toledo.

Not surprisingly, our model Burlesque show draws on the great tradition of loco locomotion. Our train is inhabited not only by the usual complement of comely PASSENGERS and toe-tapping TRAIN CONDUCTORS, but also by the dancing PRIMA DONNA who enters with a flourish midway through the number.

Here is the sequence of events:

The lights come up to reveal a drop painted to represent a train station. Enter to music the SUGAR BABIES in short nighties. They are carrying suitcases with travel labels pasted on them. They tunefully tell us that they are planning a trip on the "New Orleans Express."

"IN LOU'SIANA"

(*ORCH: 4 Bar Intro in an Easy "Swingy" 4/4*)

GIRLS.
BYE BYE! I'M PACKIN' MY GRIP
SO LONG! I'M TAKIN' A TRIP
SETTING' OUT FOR HAPPINESS
ON THE NEW ORLEANS EXPRESS

(*ORCH: 4 Bars*)

OH I WAS BORN ONE DAY
IN LOU'SIANA
GOIN' BACK TO STAY
IN LOU'SIANA
GONNA DANCE AND PLAY

IN LOU'SIANA
SO HIRE A HALL
TELL 'EM ALL
HERE I COME

I MISS THE CANDIED YAMS
IN LOU'SIANA
MISS THE SHRIMPS AND HAMS
IN LOU'SIANA
AND MY HONEYLAMB'S
IN LOU'SIANA

I'M HEADIN' BACK
CLEAR THE TRACK
HERE I COME

LET THAT WHISTLE START BLOWIN'
COME ON, THROW IN THE COAL
GET UP STEAM AND GET GOIN'
'CAUSE I'M READY TO ROLL

I MISS THE SUGAR CANE
IN LOU'SIANA
MISS THE PINK CHAMPAGNE
IN LOU'SIANA
GONNA LEAVE THIS TRAIN
IN LOU'SIANA
AN' NEVER ROAM
FROM MY HOME
WAY DOWN SOUTH

(*ORCH: 2 Bars for BOYS' entrance*)

Boys.
THE FOLKS I LEFT BEHIND
IN LOU'SIANA
ARE SO WARM AND KIND
IN LOU'SIANA
GONNA EASE MY MIND
IN LOU'SIANA
AND SETTLE DOWN
IN THE TOWN
I LOVE BEST

THE BALMY AIR IS RARE
IN LOU'SIANA
ALL THE GIRLS ARE FAIR
IN LOU'SIANA
  Girls.
MEN ARE DEBONAIR
IN LOU'SIANA
  All.
I WANNA GO
WHERE I KNOW
LIFE HAS ZEST

GOT A YEN THAT KEEPS GROWIN'
A NEW GLOW IN MY SOUL
TELLIN' ME TO GET GOIN'
NOW I'M READY TO ROLL
READY TO ROLL
READY TO R - O - L - L - L

I NEVER HAD A CARE
IN LOU'SIANA
JOY IS EVERYWHERE
IN LOU'SIANA
THERE IS LOVE TO SPARE
IN LOU'SIANA
SO SCURRY ME
HURRY ME
WAY DOWN SOUTH

(*ORCH: 14 Bar Train Transition*)

(*During this song, the SUGAR BABIES place their suitcases
on the stage and tap dance on them. They are joined shortly
by the BOYS of the GAIETY QUARTET, dressed as the
aforementioned CONDUCTORS. ALL agree that "there is
love to spare in Lou'siana." The BOYS and GIRLS exit.*
*There is a 14-bar transition during which a Train appears. This
effect should be deliberately naive, and the choreographer
has a wide choice of silly possibilities.* **

---

*NOTE: On Broadway, the train was comprised of flats on rollers painted to
represent a locomotive, six Pullmans, and an observation car. The Pullmans
were reversible and had cut-out windows. The GIRLS pushed them from R. to L.,

*The Train pulls into the station, and with an appropriate flourish
the PRIMA DONNA enters, in elegant travelling clothes.
Perhaps overjoyed at having arrived safely, she bursts into
somewhat irrelevant song.)*

"I FEEL A SONG COMING ON"

(ORCH: 6 Bar Intro)

PRIMA DONNA.
I - - - -
FEEL A SONG COMIN' ON
AND I'M WARNIN' YA
IT'S A VICTORIOUS
HAPPY AND GLORIOUS NEW STRAIN

I - - - -
FEEL A SONG COMIN' ON
IT'S A MELODY
FULL OF THE LAUGHTER
OF CHILDREN OUT AFTER THE RAIN

YOU'LL HEAR A TUNEFUL STORY
RINGIN' THRU YA
LOVE AND GLORY
HALLELUJAH!

AND NOW - - - -
THAT MY TROUBLES ARE GONE
LET THOSE HEAVENLY
DRUMS GO ON DRUMMIN'
'CAUSE I FEEL A SONG - - - -
COMIN' ON

(ORCH: 8 Bar Transition to)
*(ORCH: 35 Bar Tap Dance Section with PRIMA DONNA
    and QUARTET)*

---

showing us an interior view of the cars, then reversed at the L. proscenium, crossed
L. to R., and waved at us through the train windows. On this second cross, the
locomotive and observation car were added. After the train stopped, the CON-
DUCTORS wheeled on a baggage cart. On the cart was the PRIMA DONNA.
She was perched jauntily on some elegant, expensive luggage.

(During the second chorus, the PRIMA DONNA takes off her wrap-around skirt and taps enthusiastically, backed by the FOUR CONDUCTORS. She exits at the end of the song, and a yellow traveller closes in. She returns for an encore.)

"GOIN' BACK TO NEW ORLEANS"

(ORCH: 2 Bar Drum Intro to 8 Bar Dance Intro)

PRIMA DONNA.
GOIN' BACK TO NEW ORLEANS
WHERE THE LIVIN'S SWEET
BROUGHT MY DANCIN' SHOES TO NEW ORLEANS
GOT 'EM ON MY FEET
  BOYS.
LOVE THE JAZZ IN NEW ORLEANS
WANNA HEAR THE BAND
PLAY THAT RAZZ-MA-TAZZ
IN NEW ORLEANS
  ALL.
THAT THEY
CALL
DIXIE
LAND

(ORCH: 53 Bar Tap Dance Section to End)
(During this number she takes part in a kind of challenge-tap with the BOYS and, needless to say, struts off victorious.)

BLACKOUT

ACT ONE

SCENE 6

THE BROKEN ARMS HOTEL

In darkness, a phone rings. Lights up to reveal a shabby hotel lobby. A desk C. with two upright phones on it. CLERK is discovered behind the desk. BELLBOY is near L. proscenium. At R. is a door leading to one of the rooms.

CLERK. (*into phone*) Hello. Is this Room 19? It is. Are you the lady that left a call for ten o'clock? You are? Well, it's six o'clock. You got four more hours to sleep. (*He hangs up. Second phone rings.*) Broken Arms. Yes, Mrs. Clyde. I'll attend to it at once. (*He hangs up, rings bell.*) Oh, Tommy, there's something wrong with Mrs. Clyde's keyhole. Go upstairs and look into it.

BELLBOY. Yes, sir! (*He exits* S.L. *as phone rings again.*)

CLERK. This is the Broken Arms Hotel. Front desk. What's that? You say you've got a leak in your bathtub? Well, go right ahead. You paid for the room.

(*COMIC, looking extremely disheveled, enters from* S.R. *door. He is wearing pants with suspenders over long winter underwear.*)

COMIC. What kind of place is this?

CLERK. What's the matter, sir?

COMIC. I can't get any sleep. There's a woman two blocks away, standing at her window. And she's barefoot . . . (*indicating his head*) . . . right up to here.

CLERK. Well, if she's two blocks away, why don't you pull down the shade?

COMIC. I can't reach that far. Besides, there's a terrible racket in the room upstairs.

CLERK. Oh, I forgot to tell you, sir. They're holding an Elk's ball up there. (*A look of sympathetic pain crosses COMIC's face.*)

COMIC. Well, tell them to let the hell go, so we can get some sleep. Hey, listen, I'm checking out. I'll get my car, and I'll be right back.

(*He exits as OLD MAN and YOUNG GIRL enter. They are obviously newlyweds. He is wearing morning clothes, she an abbreviated bridal costume. He carries a suitcase.*)

OLD MAN. Come on, darlin'. (*to clerk*) I beg your pardon. Can we get a room for the night? I'd like the bridal suite. We just got married.

CLERK. Oh, honeymooners. You can have the bridal suite right over there. (indicating the room just vacated by COMIC) Did you come a long way?

YOUNG BRIDE. Yes. And now I'm ready to go a lot further.

(*starts across to* s.r. *door*) Hurry up, dear, I can hardly wait. I can hardly wait! (*She exits into the room* r. *and OLD MAN starts to follow her off.*)

OLD MAN. (*indicating his heart*) Keep pumping, pal.

CLERK. (*stopping OLD MAN*) Oh, sir. That's a very energetic young wife you have there. But there is such a difference in your ages. Couldn't a honeymoon like this prove fatal?

OLD MAN. Hey, listen. If she dies, she dies! (*He exits. Enter COMIC,* l. *He runs toward* s.r. *door.*)

COMIC. (*yelling to someone offstage*) Keep the motor running. I'll be right back. I left something in the room.

CLERK. I'm sorry, sir. You can't go in there. I just rented that room to a newly-married couple. I can't disturb them.

COMIC. I tell you, I left something in that room, and I'm gonna get it. (*He walks toward door.*) Besides, if they just got married, they won't be asleep.

OLD MAN. (*off*) Whose beautiful red lips are those, darlin'?

YOUNG BRIDE. (*off*) They're yours, Daddy.

OLD MAN. (*off*) And whose lily-white shoulders are those?

YOUNG BRIDE. (*off*) They're yours, Daddy.

OLD MAN. (*off*) And whose cute little pink tummy is that?

YOUNG BRIDE. (*off*) That's yours, Daddy.

COMIC. (*shouting at the door*) When you get to the hairbrush, that's mine. (*to CLERK*) Hey, listen, they're busy. When you find it, wrap it up and send it to me by slingshot. (*He starts to exit.*)

CLERK. (*stopping him*) Wait a minute, sir. You forgot your bill.

COMIC. My bill?

CLERK. (*presenting it*) Yes, that will be a hundred and twenty dollars.

COMIC. A hundred and twenty dollars for one night? This must be (LOCAL).*

CLERK. That's $50 for the room and $70 for the food you and your wife ordered.

COMIC. My wife didn't order any food.

CLERK. It was there if you wanted it.

COMIC. (*angrily giving CLERK some money*) Here's $50, and I'm charging you $70 for fooling around with my wife.

---

*Use the name of the town in which the show is playing.

CLERK. (*indignantly*) I didn't fool around with your wife.
COMIC. It was there if you wanted it. (*He exits* S.L.)

BLACKOUT

ACT ONE

SCENE 7

FEATHERED FANTASY

(*A Tribute to Sally Rand*)

*Needless to say, Burlesque producers could not afford the lavish
sets and costumes of the Follies. But they did try to offer
their undemanding audiences a certain (threadbare) ele-
gance and (tarnished) glamour.*
The style of this "Feathered Fantasy" is hand-me-down Ziegfeld.
*It begins in front of the blue traveller with the entrance of the
JUVENILE, a nasal tenor in white tie and tails. He sings,
somewhat stiffly, a tribute to the late Sally Rand, the most
famous fan dancer on the variety stage.*

"SALLY"

JUVENILE.
ONE LOVELY LADY
WHOSE HAIR FALLS
IN RINGLETS OF GOLD
APPEARS ON THE STAGE DISHABILLE
YET HAS NEVER CAUGHT COLD
SHE'S A GREAT SENSATION
ALL ACROSS THE NATION
DANCING WITH FANS AND BALLOONS
WHAT A SIGHT TO BEHOLD
MY DARLING

SALLY, SALLY
SWEET AND SHY
THE DREAM OF
EV'RY MAN

SALLY, SALLY
HIDES EACH THIGH
'NEATH A FEATHERED
FAN

THIS DOVE SENT FROM ABOVE
CAME TO EXCITE ME
WITH GESTURES OF INFINITE
GRACE

HER ARMS TREMBLING WITH LOVE
SEEM TO INVITE ME
TO NIGHTS FILLED WITH DELIGHTS
IN HER EMBRACE

SALLY, SALLY
FROM THE START
AS YOU DANCED I KNEW
YOU ALONE WOULD OWN MY HEART—
SALLY
I LOVE
YOU

(*ORCH: 14 Bar Intro to Dance Section*
ORCH: 32 Bar Solo Dance Section with PRINCIPAL SALLY
ORCH: 38 Bar Dance Section with FEMALE ENSEMBLE
ORCH: Return to Vocal)

JUVENILE. (*offstage*)
SALLY, SALLY
FROM THE START
AS WE KISSED I KNEW
YOU ALONE WOULD OWN MY HEART—
SALLY
I LOVE
YOU

(*Orch: 4 Bar Tag*)
(*When he comes to the end of the second chorus, the traveller
parts to reveal a blue grotto. If the designer wishes, the walls
of the grotto can be mirrors, but ordinary painted wings and
borders will suffice. Indeed, with the help of romantic and*

mysterious lighting, the number can be presented on an almost bare stage.

A spotlight catches our SALLY, a beautiful FAN DANCER, swathed at first in feathers that look like the giant wings of a beautiful night bird. During a 14-bar introduction to her solo, she emerges from the feathers. Then for 32 bars, she twirls, soars and glides across the stage. On each turn she covers her body with her fans, just in time to prevent a tantalizing glimpse of nakedness.***

Suddenly the stage is filled with OTHER FAN DANCERS (the ENSEMBLE), ALL exact copies of SALLY. In the mirror we see OTHER SALLYS, too, and for 38 bars the blue grotto is alive with these elegant winged creatures.

As the JUVENILE (offstage) sings one final chorus, the DANCERS pose c. in a spectacular pyramid of feathers, and the spot lingers for a second on our first SALLY before the BLACKOUT.)

ACT ONE

SCENE 8

THE WORLD'S GREATEST KNIFE-THROWER

ANNOUNCER. (*enters at* L. *proscenium*) Ladies and Gentlemen, please welcome to the Gaiety Theatre—that lynx-eyed mistress of the steel blade—the world's greatest knife-thrower, Miss _________________________.

(Fanfare. The PRIMA DONNA as the KNIFE-THROWER appears c. through the pink curtain. She has a whip in her belt. The curtains part to reveal at R. proscenium a knife board with the silhouette of a man painted on it. A table L., on which some knives are placed.)

---

*Either our SOUBRETTE or a featured MEMBER of the CHORUS.
**Only the illusion of nakedness. Fan dancers wore complete flesh-colored body stockings.

KNIFE-THROWER. Thank you, Ladies and Gentlemen. I need an assistant from the audience. Anyone who assists me receives a crisp new hundred dollar bill. Oh, there's a young man that needs some money. That's right, sir. Come right up here onto the stage. (*A sad-eyed COMIC climbs to the stage from the auditorium.*) Let's give this accommodating man a great big hand. (*applause, perhaps*) Thank you for coming forward.

COMIC. Glad to help. Where's my hundred dollars?

KNIFE-THROWER. (*taking a bill from her pocket and tearing it*) You get half now . . . (*gives him half*) And half when the trick is over. (*puts other half in her pocket*)

COMIC. That seems fair. (*KNIFE-THROWER guides COMIC to board. She takes a cigarette from her pocket.*)

KNIFE-THROWER. Now, sir, just stand over there . . . (*COMIC does so.*) . . . and put this cigarette in your mouth.

COMIC. Thank you very much, but I don't smoke.

KNIFE-THROWER. No, you don't understand. I'm going to stand over there and throw a knife at that cigarette.

COMIC. You're going to what?

KNIFE-THROWER. I'm going to cut that cigarette in half with my knife.

COMIC. Oh, no you're not. (*She cracks the whip.*)

KNIFE-THROWER. Back against the board. Back! (*He cowers against the board. Sharpening a knife.*) That's better. I used to have a regular assistant when I did this act before.

COMIC. Oh, you did?

KNIFE-THROWER. (*sharpening a knife*) Yes, he was a little fellow about your size. I called him little Sylvester.

COMIC. That's a nice name.

KNIFE-THROWER. But he's no longer with me. Now for my first trick.

COMIC. What happened to little Sylvester?

KNIFE-THROWER. Oh . . . well. You know how it is. Ladies and Gentlemen, for my first display of skill . . .

COMIC. (*more firmly*) What happened to little Sylvester?

KNIFE-THROWER. Well, if you must know, one night between shows, I had an argument with that Bulgarian son of a gypsy who calls himself my husband, and I was a little nervous. I was getting ready to throw a knife at little Sylvester's cigarette and I missed the cigarette. The press was very unkind. I didn't miss by much. What's a few inches more or less after all these years?

COMIC. (*starts to go*) So long. I'll see you later.

KNIFE-THROWER. (*her hand shaking*) No, come back. You see, that night my hand was shaking. My hand doesn't shake any more.

COMIC. It doesn't shake any less, either.

KNIFE-THROWER. Remember the hundred dollars.

COMIC. It's a good thing for you that I'm greedy. (*goes to board*)

KNIFE-THROWER. Are you ready?

COMIC. Yes.

KNIFE-THROWER. Are you against the board?

COMIC. Yes, I'm against the . . . You can't see the board? You're going to throw a knife at that board and you can't see it?

KNIFE-THROWER. I'm not throwing at the board. I'm throwing at the cigarette.

COMIC. (*laughs*) That's right. (*to audience*) The board's got nothing to do with it.

KNIFE-THROWER. Are you ready?

COMIC. Yes.

KNIFE-THROWER. Are you against the board?

COMIC. Yes.

KNIFE-THROWER. Is the cigarette in your mouth?

COMIC. Yes, it's in my . . . (*He stops short.*) You can't see the cigarette? You're going to throw a knife at the cigarette and you can't see it?

KNIFE-THROWER. (*myopically*) Keep talking. I'll find you. Are you ready?

COMIC. Yeah.

KNIFE-THROWER. You're against the board? You've got the cigarette in your mouth?

COMIC. Yes.

KNIFE-THROWER. Here we go. One . . . Two . . . Wait! Wait!

COMIC. What now?

KNIFE-THROWER. I've got a better idea. Turn and face me. (*COMIC faces her, his cigarette dangling from his mouth.*) Ladies and Gentlemen, tonight I am going to perform the most difficult feat ever attempted by a knife-thrower. I'm going to throw and split that cigarette right down the middle.

COMIC. Hey . . . that is a terrific shot! Don't miss this, folks. She's going to split that cigarette down the middle . . . (*sudden realization*) . . . and split my head right with it. I'll see you later, sister.

KNIFE-THROWER. What's the matter?

COMIC. I'm going home. I forgot something.
KNIFE-THROWER. What did you forget?
COMIC. I forgot to stay there.
KNIFE-THROWER. No. Come back. You're right. I'll play it safe.
COMIC. (*stopping*) You will?
KNIFE-THROWER. Sure. I'll do it exactly as I did it with little Sylvester.
COMIC. Well, that's better.
KNIFE-THROWER. Ready. (*a fanfare*) One . . . two . . . three. (*throws first knife which lands near the COMIC's ankle*) Oops. Missed. (*She throws a second knife which just misses his shoulder.*) Getting closer. (*The third knife misses the board and we hear a scream offstage. A pause.*) Completely missed the board. (*A fourth knife whizzes past the COMIC's ear.*) That's better. (*The last knife catches the board right between the comic's legs. HE is paralyzed with fear.*) Ladies and Gentlemen, there stands a brave man. The man I've been waiting for all my life. Come to my arms, my prince, my hero.
COMIC. (*high voice*) I can't.
KNIFE-THROWER. Oh yes, you can, my death-defying darling. I want what I want when I want it, and right now I want it.
COMIC. You'll get what I've got when I've got it, and right now I ain't got it.

BLACKOUT

ACT ONE

SCENE 9

ELLIS ISLAND LOVE STORY

Burlesque comedians prided themselves on their versatility, and the 1ST COMIC here is given a chance to wring a tear or two from the eyes of his hard-headed, soft-hearted audience.
He enters in One with the GAIETY QUARTET. In perfect*

---

*Nearly all Columbia Wheel Burlesque shows had quartets to support the principal comedian in his specialty turn. Among the more prominent examples are the Church City Boys in Louis Robie's *Knickerbockers* and The Four Harmonists in *The Girls From Happyland.*

harmony they tell us the story of a little immigrant girl who is seeking an old love in the New World.

"IMMIGRATION ROSE"

(*ORCH: 8 Bar Intro*)

1ST COMIC. (*solo, ad lib*) QUARTET. (*hums background*)

DOWN AT ELLIS ISLAND
WHERE THE SHIPS COME IN
FROM EVERYWHERE ACROSS THE SEA
SITS A LITTLE GIRL
WITH HEAVY HEART WITHIN
WAITING FOR SOMEONE SO ANXIOUSLY
QUARTET. (*answering*)
SO ANXIOUSLY
1ST COMIC.
SEARCHES EV'RY FACE
BUT ALL IN VAIN
QUARTET.
SHE SEARCHES VAINLY
1ST COMIC.
WILL SHE HAVE TO GO BACK HOME AGAIN
QUARTET.
TO HER LOVED ONES

(*ORCH: Chorus, In Tempo*)

1ST COMIC.
ROSE
QUARTET.
THE ONE HE CHOSE
1ST COMIC.
LITTLE IMMIGRATION ROSE
QUARTET.
WITH TURNED UP NOSE
1ST COMIC.
IN HER EUROPEAN CLOTHES
QUARTET.
SHE NEARLY FROZE
1ST COMIC.
NOT BY PEERAGE

SHE CAME STEERAGE
AND NOW
 Quartet.
IT'S SAD TO TELL
 1st Comic.
THERE'S NOBODY WITH A HELPING HAND
 Quartet.
NO ONE
 1st Comic.
THAT SHE CAN UNDERSTAND
 All.
HAS SHE COME TO THIS LAND
 1st Comic. (*ad lib*)
TO BE DEPORTED

(ORCH: Back to Tempo)

 1st Comic (*continued*)
TEARS
 Quartet.
THAT START SO SMALL
 1st Comic.
START APPEARING IN HER EYES
 Quartet.
THEY START TO FALL
 1st Comic.
WHEN SHE HEARS SOMEBODY CRY
 Quartet.
SHE HEARS HIM CALL
 1st Comic.
"ROSIE, DARLING, HERE AM I!"
 Quartet.
"HERE AM I YOUR TEARS TO DRY!"
 1st Comic.
HE HOLDS HER CLOSE—
TO HIS HEART FOR HE KNOWS—
 All.
IN THIS LAND THAT SHE CHOSE
WILL BLOOM HIS IMMIGRATION ROSE—

(*ORCH: Melody played as 1ST COMIC and QUARTET sing
 Counter Melody*)

ALL.
WHEN SHE PASSED MISS LIBERTY
SHE HAD REACHED HER DESTINY
AND HER HEART WAS BEATING FAST
HE WAS WAITING THERE AT LAST
TO HOLD HER CLOSE
TO HIS HEART
FOR HE KNOWS
IN THIS LAND THAT SHE CHOSE
   1ST COMIC. (*solo, ad lib*)
WILL BLOOM HIS IMMIGRATION
ROSE
   QUARTET.
THAT LOVELY ROSE
   1ST COMIC. (*spoken*) Rose?

(*ORCH: Chord*)
(*The lovers of the song are united. Our robust melodists end
   on an appropriate note of joy.*)

BLACKOUT

ACT ONE

SCENE 10

SCENES FROM DOMESTIC LIFE

*Five Blackouts in one. Traveller closed. No pause between these
   brief scenes.*

a. *"Burglar"*

(*Sirens, shots. Spotlights pick up SOUBRETTE in short nightgown and 2ND COMIC fully dressed. They are running,
   and she is hollering, "Police, Police." They cross each
   other twice, then 2ND COMIC stops her near L. proscenium.*)

2ND COMIC. Wait a minute, dear. Wait a minute. What's the
matter?

SOUBRETTE. Don't stop me, Jimmy. There was a burglar at our house.

2ND COMIC. A burglar at our house? Did he get anything?

SOUBRETTE. Yes. I thought it was you.

CHORD. BLACKOUT

b. *"Betting"*

(*Spot picks up CHARACTER MAN (JACK) near* R. *proscenium. 2ND COMIC, who has remained onstage, walks into CHARACTER MAN's light.*)

CHARACTER. I hear you are a betting man, Jimmy.

2ND COMIC. I've been known to make a little wager.

CHARACTER. Well, I'll bet you twenty dollars that I can answer any question you ask me.

2ND COMIC. That's a bet. And to prove I'm a sport, I'll bet five dollars I can answer any question you ask me.

CHARACTER. It's a bet.

2ND COMIC. All right. What is it that has four legs, four feathers, flies upside down like an Australian twilly bird and yodels every other Tuesday?

CHARACTER. Damned if I know. (*hands him bill*) Here's your twenty.

2ND COMIC. Thanks.

CHARACTER. By the way, what is it?

2ND COMIC. Damned if I know. (*hands him bill*) Here's your five.

CHORD. BLACKOUT

c. *"Philadelphia"*

(*Spotlight discovers VILLAIN (STRAIGHT) in frock coat, standing over seated FATHER (2ND CHARACTER MAN) near* L. *proscenium*)

VILLAIN. Well, the mortgage is three months overdue, and I won't wait a day longer.

FATHER. Just give me a little more time. My daughter, little Nell, is coming back today. And she promised she'd bring the money. (*auto horn offstage*) Here's little Nell now.

(*enter NELL [SOUBRETTE], dressed modestly but attractively*)

FATHER. (*continued*) Oh, Nell, thank God you're here. The interest on the mortgage is due.
NELL. Never mind the interest. How much is the principal?
VILLAIN. Three thousand dollars.
NELL. Here's your money. (*hands him money, takes paper from him, hands paper to FATHER*) Here's your mortgage. (*to VILLAIN again*) Now get. (*He exits* R.)
FATHER. Oh, Nell, I knew you wouldn't fail us. But where did you get the money?
NELL. In Philadelphia.
FATHER. In Philadelphia? You got three thousand dollars in Philadelphia? Look at me, little Nell, and tell me: Have you been good?
NELL. To get three thousand dollars in Philadelphia, you've got to be good.

CHORD. BLACKOUT

d. *"Dutiful Daughters"*

(*Lights up to reveal THREE DAUGHTERS in party dresses near* R. *proscenium. To the* L. *of them CHARACTER MAN as their FATHER is sitting in a rocking chair, reading a newspaper. In unison, they clear their throats. He lowers his newspaper.*)

FATHER. Yes?
THREE DAUGHTERS. (*in unison*)
FATHER, DEAR FATHER, DON'T STAY UP LATE.
IT'S FRIDAY NIGHT, AND WE'VE EACH GOT A DATE.
1ST DAUGHTER.
I'VE GOT A DATE WITH A GUY NAMED JOE
HE'S GOING TO TAKE ME TO A PICTURE SHOW.
FATHER. Have a good time, dear. (*1ST DAUGHTER curtsies and exits.*)
2ND DAUGHTER.
I'VE GOT A DATE WITH A GUY NAMED PETE.
WE'RE GOING TO THE RITZ TO GET SOMETHING TO EAT.
FATHER. Have a good time, dear. (*2ND DAUGHTER curtsies and exits.*)

3RD DAUGHTER.
I HAVE A DATE WITH A GUY NAMED CHUCK . . .
FATHER. (*sharply*) You get right upstairs and go to bed.

CHORD. BLACKOUT

e. *"Monkey Business"*

(*Spotlight picks up POLICEMAN and SOUBRETTE next to an open window. She is wearing the POLICEMAN's coat and apparently nothing else. HE is taking notes in his shirt sleeves.*)

SOUBRETTE. Thank you, Officer, for lending me your coat. It was getting very drafty up here.

POLICEMAN. You're welcome, Miss. Now can you tell me just what happened here.

SOUBRETTE. Well, my boss, Mr. Gilmore, just jumped out of the window and it's twenty stories down.

POLICEMAN. Who are you?

SOUBRETTE. Well, I'm his private secretary. I take dictation, I type. I lick stamps.

POLICEMAN. Was there anything odd about Mr. Gilmore's behavior today?

SOUBRETTE. Well, he always was a bit peculiar. I had only been working here three days when he burst into the office one morning in a terrible state. "Miss Jones," he said, "You're the most beautiful creature I've ever seen in my life. If I give you a hundred dollars, will you stand before me in your slip. I promise you, there'll be no monkey business." Well, Officer, to a working girl a hundred dollars is a lot of money.

POLICEMAN. Of course it is.

SOUBRETTE. So I took the money and stood before him in my slip. And it was a cute slip. It had a plunging neckline and was cut way up to here . . .

POLICEMAN. (*interrupting her*) Was he as good as his word?

SOUBRETTE. Yes, there was no monkey business.

POLICEMAN. Did that satisfy him?

SOUBRETTE. It did until a week ago.

POLICEMAN. What happened then?

SOUBRETTE. He burst into the office again. And he was a sorry sight. His tie was askew; his eyes were rimmed with red. "Miss

Jones, he said, "I can't get your face out of my mind. If I give you two hundred dollars, will you stand before me in your panties and your brassiere. I promise there'll be no monkey business." Well, Officer, to a working girl, two hundred dollars is a lot of money . . .

POLICEMAN. Of course it is.

SOUBRETTE. So, I took the money and stood before him in my pants and brassiere. (*rattling on*) Well, I did look cute, I had a big red heart down here (*indicating pants*) and tassels—one turned this way . . . one turned that . . .

POLICEMAN. (*interrupting her*) Was he as good as his word?

SOUBRETTE. Yes, there was no monkey business.

POLICEMAN. Did that satisfy him?

SOUBRETTE. Until ten minutes ago.

POLICEMAN. What happened then?

SOUBRETTE. Oh, he pushed open the door and he looked just awful. "Miss Jones," he said, "I'm spending sleepless nights because of you. If I pay you five hundred dollars, will you stand before me in the nude . . . I promise there'll be no monkey business." Well, Officer, to a working girl, five hundred dollars is a lot of money . . .

POLICEMAN. Of course it is.

SOUBRETTE. So I removed my clothes and stood before him in the nude. "Miss Jones," he said, "I can't stand it anymore. How much is the monkey business?"

POLICEMAN. Yes?

SOUBRETTE. And when I told him my regular price was ten dollars, he jumped out of the window.

CHORD. BLACKOUT

ACT ONE

SCENE 11

TORCH SONG

The PRIMA DONNA must have a specialty in the First Act, and here we present her in a number borrowed from Ed Wynn. A spotlight catches her face as she is perched on top of an upright piano near the R. *proscenium.*

"DON'T BLAME ME"

(*ORCH: 4 Bar Intro*)

    PRIMA DONNA. (*ad lib*)
EVER SINCE THE LUCKY NIGHT I FOUND YOU
I HUNG AROUND YOU
JUST LIKE A FOOL
FALLING HEAD IN HEELS IN LOVE
LIKE A KID OUT OF SCHOOL

MY POOR HEART IS IN AN AWFUL STATE NOW
BUT IT'S TOO LATE NOW
TO CALL A HALT
SO IF I BECOME A NUISANCE
IT'S ALL YOUR FAULT

(*ORCH: 4 Bars in "Easy" Tempo*)

(*As she sings, the lights widen. Surprise! The piano has bicycle wheels. A deadpan ACCOMPANIST (one of the MALE ENSEMBLE) pedals the piano and, therefore, the PRIMA DONNA back and forth across the stage. She is perfectly at ease and takes no notice of the incongruity of her situation.*)

DON'T BLAME ME
FOR FALLING IN LOVE WITH YOU
I'M UNDER YOUR SPELL
BUT HOW CAN I HELP IT
DON'T BLAME ME

CAN'T YOU SEE
WHEN YOU DO THE THINGS YOU DO
IF I CAN'T CONCEAL
THE THRILL THAT I'M FEELING
DON'T BLAME ME

I CAN'T HELP IT
IF THAT DOGGONE MOON
ABOVE
MAKES ME NEED
SOMEONE LIKE YOU
TO LOVE

BLAME YOUR KISS
AS SWEET AS A KISS CAN BE
AND BLAME ALL YOUR CHARMS
THAT MELT IN MY ARMS
BUT DON'T BLAME ME

(*ORCH: Melody of the release is played as PRIMA DONNA
   sings Counter Melody.*)

BLAME THAT MOON
UP ABOVE
MAKING ME NEED
SOMEONE
LIKE YOU TO
LOVE

(*ORCH: Back to Melody*)

BLAME YOUR KISS
AS SWEET AS A KISS CAN BE
AND BLAME ALL YOUR CHARMS

(*ORCH: 1 Bar Fill*)

THAT MELT IN MY ARMS

(*ORCH: 1 Bar Fill*)

BUT DON'T —

(*ORCH: Sweeping Crescendo*)

BLAME —

(*ORCH: Back to Tempo*)

ME —

(*ORCH: 4 Bar Orch Ending, Big to a Hold. On her climactic
   holding note, she is wheeled triumphantly off left into the
   wings.*)

BLACKOUT

SUGAR BABIES
ACT ONE

SCENE 12

ORIENTALE

*There were no strips in early Burlesque, but there were Kooch
dances, 'Salome' dances, and other tantalizing celebrations
of female sexuality.*
*That tradition is represented in SUGAR BABIES by a tribute to
Little Egypt and La Sylphe, the two most famous hip-shak-
ers on the variety stage.*
*The scene begins with the discovery near the L. proscenium of
the CHARACTER MAN, here serving as ANNOUNCER.*

ANNOUNCER. (*after drum roll*) Here she is, Ladies and Gentlemen . . . held over for the twenty-first week . . . (*consulting
a card as if to refresh a faulty memory*) that sensation of the
World's Fair . . . with the dance that made Damascus sizzle . . .
Little Cairo, herself . . . the teasing, the tempting, the tantalizing Christina.*

(*A spotlight comes on suddenly to discover, C., an attractive
BELLY DANCER, veiled and bejewelled. She shakes and
quivers to some pseudo-Arabian music.** The dance is in
three parts: 32 bars of an enthusiastic introduction, a 12-bar
shimmy to percussion only; and a spectacular 32-bar finale.
If convenient, use a glitter ball to add excitement to the last
moments of the dance.*)

BLACKOUT

---

*NOTE: Substitute the performer's own name. The dancer can be the SOU-
BRETTE or, if more appropriate, a featured member of the ensemble.
**NOTE: Actually, arrangements of other tunes in the show, notably *"SALLY"*
and *"CUBAN LOVE SONG."* See orchestra score.

ACT ONE

Scene 13

THE LITTLE RED SCHOOLHOUSE

ORCHESTRA plays a signature tune. Curtain parts to reveal schoolroom with teacher's desk and four smaller desks for pupils. TEACHER is discovered. She is wearing a schoolmarm dress. She has a rolled newspaper in her hands. TWO GIRLS enter. They are dressed as third graders and wear pigtails. TEACHER rings the bell.

Teacher. Good morning, girls.
Girls. Good morning, Teacher.
Teacher. Where is Jimmy Matthews?

(2ND COMIC enters as CHILD. He is wearing a middy blouse and knickers.)

2nd Comic. Here I am, Teach. Hey, Teach, before class starts, may I ask you a question?
Teacher. Certainly, Jimmy.
2nd Comic. Can an eleven-year-old girl have a baby?
Teacher. Certainly not.
2nd Comic. (*to 1ST GIRL as he sits*) See, honey, I told you we had nothing to worry about.
Teacher. All right, children. Class will come to order. Where is Mickey Yule?

(1ST COMIC, wearing short pants, a curly wig and a little cap, enters.)

1st Comic. Here I am, Teach. Sorry I'm late, but I got held up in traffic. A little dog was broken down.
Teacher. Broken down?
1st Comic. Yeah, but another little dog was pushing him home.
Teacher. Did you bring a note from your mother and father explaining why you're late?
1st Comic. My mother and father were having an argument.

TEACHER. Who's your father?
1ST COMIC. That's what they were arguing about.

(*TEACHER hits 1ST COMIC with her newspaper. This piece of business recurs throughout the scene, and 1ST COMIC ad libs a variety of responses to it.*)

TEACHER. All right, class. Come to order. Mickey.
1ST COMIC. Yes, Teach.
TEACHER. Did you finish your arithmetic homework last night?
1ST COMIC. Yes, I added those figures ten times.
TEACHER. Good boy.
1ST COMIC. And here are the ten answers. (*TEACHER hits him. Perhaps he says, "That cleared up my sinuses."*)
TEACHER. That's enough of arithmetic. Now it's time for history. Tell me, Rosie. What happened in the year 1898?
2ND GIRL. (*standing*) The battleship Maine was sunk. (*The PUPILS congratulate her. She curtsies into her seat.*)
TEACHER. Very good, Rosie. Now, Mickey, tell me what happened in the year 1900.
1ST COMIC. (*standing*) The battleship Maine was sunk two years. (*TEACHER hits 1ST COMIC.*) I was six-foot-one when I came in here. (*HE whines softly, sits, then feels 2ND GIRL's leg. 2ND GIRL slaps his hand coquettishly.*)
TEACHER. That's certainly enough of history. Now it's time for our English lesson. (*The PUPILS ad lib, "Good," "I like English," etc.*) Jimmy, use the words "defense," "defeat," and "detail" in a sentence.
2ND COMIC. De dog jumped over *de fence*, and *de feat* went over before *de tail.*
1ST COMIC. De-pressing. (*TEACHER hits 1ST COMIC. He whines, ad libs, "What did you hit me for? He's the one who said it," etc. He sits and again plays with 2ND GIRL's leg.*)
TEACHER. All right, Mickey, give us a sentence using the word "disaster."
1ST COMIC. My girl backed into an airplane propeller. Disaster. (*TEACHER hits 1ST COMIC, knocks his wig off. He reaches for wig us., while TEACHER keeps hitting him. He gets the wig back on, but crookedly.*) Wait until I screw my head back on.
TEACHER. Now it's time for poetry.

1ST GIRL. I love poetry.

2ND COMIC. You're the type that would.

TEACHER. Diane, do you have one?

1ST GIRL. (*jumping up to recite*)
THERE WAS AN OLD WOMAN
WHO LIVED IN A SHOE.
SHE HAD NO CHILDREN
SHE KNEW WHAT TO DO.

1ST COMIC. What's the address of that shoe? (*TEACHER hits 1ST COMIC.*)

TEACHER. If you keep this up, Mickey, I'm going to hold you after school, take down your pants and spank your little bottom.

1ST COMIC. You keep promisin' but nothin' ever happens. (*TEACHER hits 1ST COMIC.*)

2ND COMIC. (*raises hand*) Hey, Teach, can I go to the boy's room?

TEACHER. Certainly, Jimmy. You're excused.

1ST COMIC. Hey, go for me, willya?

2ND COMIC. Sure, Mickey. (*2ND COMIC exits.*)

TEACHER. Do you have one, Mickey?

1ST COMIC. (*as 2ND GIRL grabs at him*) I had one when I came in.

TEACHER. Well, let's hear it.

1ST COMIC.
A BOY STOOD ON THE BURNING DECK
EATIN' PEANUTS BY THE PECK
ALONG CAME A LITTLE GIRL IN BLUE
SHE SAID, "I WISH I HAD A PECK OR TWO."

(*TEACHER hits 1ST COMIC. He picks up a newspaper from her desk. They duel briefly. He rings her bell, then sits.*)

2ND COMIC. (*returning*) Well, I went.

1ST COMIC. Did you go for me?

2ND COMIC. You didn't have to go. Teach, I've got a little one.

1ST COMIC. You're telling me.

2ND COMIC. Well, it was cold that day when we went swimmin'. Here goes.
I KNOW A GIRL
FROM BOSTON, MASS.
SHE WADED IN WATER
CLEAR UP TO HER KNEES.

TEACHER. That doesn't rhyme.

2ND COMIC. It will when the tide comes in. (*1ST COMIC laughs, shakes 2ND COMIC's hand as if to congratulate him. TEACHER hits 1ST COMIC.*)

TEACHER. That brings us to the lesson of the day. Mickey, what's the difference between prose and poetry.

1ST COMIC. That's easy. The pros stand on the corner.

TEACHER. Well, obviously you don't know; so I'll have to explain.

MY GIRL RAN ROUND THE MULBERRY BUSH,
AND I RAN ROUND TO MEET HER.
THAT LITTLE GIRL WILL NEVER KNOW
HOW GLAD I WAS TO GREET HER.

1ST COMIC. What's that?

TEACHER. That's poetry. It rhymes.

1ST COMIC. I see. Meet her, greet her. It rhymes. (*PUPILS agree.*)

TEACHER. But if I were to say,

MY GIRL WENT ROUND THE MULBERRY BUSH,
AND I WENT ROUND TO MEET HER.
THAT LITTLE GIRL WILL NEVER KNOW
HOW GLAD I FELT THAT DAY.

1ST COMIC. What's that?

TEACHER. That's prose. You see, it doesn't rhyme.

1ST COMIC. Oh. I see. Poetry rhymes and prose doesn't. (*PUPILS nod assent.*) Is that all there is to it?

TEACHER. That's all.

1ST COMIC. May I give the class an example?

TEACHER. Please do.

1ST COMIC.

MY GIRL RAN ROUND THE MULBERRY BUSH,
AND I RAN ROUND TO MEET HER.
SHE PULLED UP HER PETTICOAT
AND I PULLED OUT MY . . .

Now, what do you want? Prose or poetry?

CHORD. BLACKOUT

ACT ONE

Scene 14

PRESENTING THE SPRINGBOARD SISTERS
(WHO SING IN ALL THE DIVES)

Sister acts, seldom comprised of real siblings, were popular on the variety stage. This brief number is a tribute to such famous Burlesquers of the past as The Watsons and The O'Connor Sisters.
Enter the SOUBRETTE and TWO SISTER SUGAR BABIES through the central opening in the pink traveller. They are not overdressed.

"THE SUGAR BABY BOUNCE"

SOUBRETTE, TWO SUGAR BABIES

All.
THERE'S A NEW DANCE
SWEEPING THE NATION
YOU DANCE
FULL OF ELATION
DO DANCE
LET 'EM ALL SEE YOUR STUFF

MISTER
WHO CAN RESIST IT
SISTER
TODDLE AND TWIST IT
NO ONE
EVER CAN GET ENOUGH

(*ORCH: Chorus*)

BOOM, BAM
WIGGLE YOUR BOTTOM
FLIP, FLOP
JIGGLE YOUR TOP
DOIN' THE SUGAR BABY BOUNCE

THERE'S NOTHIN' TO IT
DO IT

IT'S JOLLITY
FRIVOLITY
TAKE IT
SHAKE IT
IT'S GLORIOUS
UPROARIOUS

CHEST OUT
SHOW 'EM YOU GOT 'EM
NO DOUBT
BUTTONS'LL POP
GIVE 'EM A THRILL
WITH EVERY OUNCE

   1ST SUGAR BABY.
NEVER BE COY
   2ND SUGAR BABY.
NEVER BE SHY
   SOUBRETTE.
GIVE 'EM THAT BOOM BOOM
RIGHT IN THE EYE
   ALL.
OOH!
DO THAT SUGAR BABY BOUNCE

(*ORCH: Counter-Melody*)

LADDY
DADDY
DON'T BE AFRAID
DO THAT
SUGAR-BABY BOUNCE
THAT WIGGLIN'
THAT JIGGLIN'
DRIVES 'EM WILD
COME TAKE IT
COME SHAKE IT
ANGEL CHILD

LADDY
DADDY
HANDLE WITH CARE
TAKE IT
BUT PLEASE DON'T BREAK IT

OH BABY
NEVER
EVER
DROP IT
OR FORSAKE IT
JUST
DO
THAT SUGAR BABY BOUNCE

(*24 Bar Dance Section:*)

   1st Sugar Baby.
NEVER BE COY
   2nd Sugar Baby.
NEVER BE SHY
   Soubrette.
GIVE 'EM THAT BOOM BOOM
RIGHT IN THE EYE
   1st Sugar Baby.
OOH
   2nd Sugar Baby.
OOH
   Soubrette.
OOH

(*5 Bar Dance Section:*)

Soubrette.	Sugar Babies.
BOOM, BAM	LADDY
WIGGLE YOUR BOTTOM	DADDY
FLIP, FLOP	DON'T BE
JIGGLE YOUR TOP –	AFRAID
DOIN' THAT	DO THAT
SUGAR-BABY BOUNCE	SUGAR BABY BOUNCE

THERE'S NOTHIN' TO IT   THAT WIGGLIN'
DO IT   THAT JIGGLIN'
IT'S JOLLITY   DRIVES 'EM
FRIVOLITY   WILD
TAKE IT   COME TAKE IT
SHAKE IT   COME SHAKE IT
IT'S GLORIOUS   ANGEL
UPROARIOUS   CHILD

CHEST OUT   LADDY
SHOW 'EM YOU GOT 'EM   DADDY
NO DOUBT   HANDLE WITH
BUTTONS'LL POP   CARE
GIVE 'EM A THRILL   TAKE IT
WITH EV'RY OUNCE   BUT PLEASE DON'T
                          BREAK IT

SOUBRETTE.
NEVER BE COY
  SUGAR BABIES.
NEVER BE SHY
  ALL THREE.
GIVE 'EM THAT BOOM BOOM
RIGHT IN THE EYE
COME ON
BABY
DON'T SAY
MAYBE
TO THAT
SUG - AR
BA - BY
BOU - - - NCE!
B - O - U - N - C - E
Bounce!
I SAID, "BOUNCE!"

(*The dance ends, as you might expect, with a most satisfactory
    triple bounce.*)

BLACKOUT

ACT ONE

SCENE 15

SPECIAL ADDED ATTRACTION:
MADAME RENTZ AND HER ALL-FEMALE
MINSTREL SHOW

The finale of our First Act commemorates a famous variety troupe—the Rentz Company founded by M. B. Leavitt in the late nineteenth century. Leavitt was a great innovator. It was he who first had the notion of adding sex to the minstrel show by substituting beautiful women in tights for the usual black-face clowns and singers. The idea was fresh in 1871, less so in the twenties. But in Burlesque nothing could stop an idea that had outlived its usefulness. And minstrelsy remained a popular theme for musical numbers until 1928. Here we make the familiar conventions a frame for two star turns: a humorous transvestite monologue by the 1st COMIC and some spectacular solo dancing by our INTERLOCU-TOR, the PRIMA DONNA.

Enter the CHARACTER MAN. He stands c. in front of the pink traveller.

CHARACTER. (*as ANNOUNCER*) Ladies and Gentlemen, the ladies of the chorus have made another lightning change of costume and are ready for the finale of the First Act, which will be familiar to all habituees of the Gaiety Theatre, not to mention you sons of habituees. It is, in fact, the longest-running act on the variety stage—Madame Rentz and her all-female minstrel show . . .

(Curtains part to reveal the FOURTEEN SUGAR BABIES in a minstrel pose. The GIRLS are wearing tights, red velvet jackets, and top hats. They all have tambourines. Behind them is a platform on which are seats for an INTERLOCUTOR and CHORUS. Beside each seat is a banjo. The drop, which completes the scene, is painted to represent the stage furnishings of a nineteenth-century concert hall. Minstrel Sequence)

"DOWN AT THE GAIETY BURLESQUE"

(*In this song the GIRLS invite us to Madame Rentz's Minstrel
    Show and introduce the INTERLOCUTOR who is our
    PRIMA DONNA. SHE enters mid-song, dressed in white
    tie, white formal jacket, white top hat, tights and boots.*)

GIRLS.
IF YOU'RE WORKING TOO HARD
THEN LEAVE THE WORK ON YOUR DESK
MEET US AT THE GAIETY BURLESQUE

TAKE YOUR MIND OFF YOUR BIZ'NESS
PUT YOUR MIND ON SOME FUN
WE'VE GOT SOMETHING FOR EV'RYONE

(*ORCH: 1 Bar*)

THERE'LL BE SINGIN' AND DANCIN'
TO THE SONGS YOU HOLD DEAR
"BONES" AND "TAMBO"
BOTH WILL APPEAR

GOT A NEW INTERLOCUTOR
WITH BEAUTY AND GRACE
FOR ENJOYMENT
THIS IS THE PLACE
GET READY

(*PRIMA DONNA enters* C.S.)
HERE SHE COMES NOW
— GIVE A CHEER
MEET THE VERY LATEST ATTRACTION
SHE'S THE NEW SENSATION
— OF THE YEAR
HERE AT THE GAIETY BURLESQUE
    PRIMA DONNA. (*solo*)
ALL THE LADIES ARE WELCOME
'CAUSE THE SHOW'S NICE AN' CLEAN
JUST GOOD SPORT THERE'S
NOTHING OBSCENE

ALL THE GIRLS IN THE CHORUS LINE
ARE SHY AND DEMURE

ABSOLUTELY
WHOLESOME AND PURE!
  ALL.
GLAD YOU BROUGHT YOUR
— FAV'RITE BEAU
TO THE VERY
LATEST ATTRACTION
MADAME RENT-ZES FEMALE
— MINSTREL SHOW
HERE AT
THE GAI - E - TY
BUR -
LESQUE

(*ORCH: Hold 10 Counts*)

  PRIMA DONNA.
LADIES, BE SEATED!

(*ORCH: Chord*)

*The song ends with a crash of tambourines. TWELVE of the
GIRLS are already at their chair. TWO GIRLS as "End
Men" (i.e., TAMBO and BONES remain DS.)*

PRIMA DONNA. (*as INTERLOCUTOR*) Ladies, be seated.
(*ALL do, except TAMBO and BONES.*) Welcome, Sister Bones,
and welcome, Sister Tambourine.

TAMBO & BONES. Welcome, Madame Interlocutor.

INTERLOCUTOR. Where is your wayward sister, the Countess
Stoopandtakeit?

TAMBO. As usual, she's out looking for a man.

INTERLOCUTOR. Is she looking for any man in particular?

BONES. No, she's looking for a man who ain't particular.

INTERLOCUTOR. Well, I guess she didn't find one, 'cause here
she comes now.

(*Enter 1ST COMIC as HORTENSE, an aging chorus girl. He
wears a garish dress and a blonde wig.*)

HORTENSE. I'm sorry I'm late, Madame Interlocutor, but I was
down at the docks again, saying farewell to the brave men who
guard our shores.

INTERLOCUTOR. That was kind of you, Countess.

HORTENSE. It's my favorite charity—naval relief. (*a rattle of tambourines from the CHORUS*)

INTERLOCUTOR. That's a beautiful dress you're wearing, Countess.

HORTENSE. Yes, isn't it. (*lifts skirt to reveal a black garter*) What do you think of my garters? They cost me fifteen thousand francs in Paris.

INTERLOCUTOR. Very racy. But your dress is so gay. Why are your garters black?

HORTENSE. In memory of those who passed above. (*tambourines again*)

INTERLOCUTOR. Ah, memories. I'm sure yours are legion. Would you care to share them with us, Countess?

HORTENSE. I'll share my heartaches, yes.

INTERLOCUTOR. It will ease the pain. (*INTERLOCUTOR moves us. to her appointed chair, as HORTENSE comes forward to tell her troubles to the audience. While HORTENSE speaks, the ORCHESTRA softly plays sentimental music.*)

SOLO TURN BY HORTENSE

HORTENSE. My name is Hortense . . . Well, it is. (*Throughout, she treats laughter as an insult and pretends to be hurt by it. However, after this first line, a shill sometimes whistles, whereupon HORTENSE replies, "It takes one to know one."*) I came from a large family. Fifteen in the family, ALL CHILDREN. My father used to say to me, "Listen, Stupid," HE ALWAYS CALLED ME LISTEN. "Why don't you get a job, SO AT LEAST WE'LL KNOW WHAT KIND OF WORK YOU'RE OUT OF." I said, "I've tried, Papa, but life is hard. I'm gonna run away from home. I'm gonna run, do you hear." And he said, "ON YOUR MARK . . . GET SET . . ." I joined a dance troupe. Well, I did. I danced on my right leg. I danced on my left leg, AND BETWEEN THE TWO OF THEM I MADE A LOT OF MONEY. Our little troupe was invited to entertain the soldiers at Fort Knox. And the boys were so polite. I wore my most provocative dress. And when I walked through the barracks ALL THE PRIVATES STOOD UP. The head Colonel fell in love with me. "Hortense," he said, "will you grace my presence at the military ball." I said, "Silly goose, of course I will." He wore his medals, and I wore my organdy gown. We sipped champagne and we danced. We sipped and danced. He held me close . . . closer . . . closer . . . AND THEN HE WENT OFF IN HIS UNIFORM AND I NEVER SAW HIM AGAIN. After I lost my colonel, LIFE WAS A DRAG. Not that I lacked for lovers. There was old Judge Deadwood. He was sixty. I was twenty-two. "I'm a regular Don Juan," he said, and he spoke the truth. AFTER ONE HE WAS DONE. Then lightning struck. The once-in-a-lifetime man came into my life. Brock Allison the Ketchup King. We met in a speakeasy. He poured me a glass of whiskey. "Say when," he said, and I said, "AS SOON AS I FINISH THE WHISKEY." It was a whirlwind courtship. And Brock was so generous in his own way. He asked me what I wanted for an engagement present. And I said, "Pearls . . . pearls . . . pearls." SO HE GAVE ME A BUSHEL OF OYSTERS AND WISHED ME LUCK." And on our wedding day he gave me a nightgown with fur around the bottom. "What's the fur for?" I said. And he replied, "TO KEEP YOUR NECK WARM." That night when the wedding guests had gone, he took me tenderly in his arms. "Tell me, Hortense," he whispered. "Am I the first?" And I said, "WHY DOES EVERYBODY ASK ME THAT?" For some reason Brock became moody, business took him to Europe. He deserted me. I was alone again. I was driven to drink. I FORGOT WHO DROVE ME. I became a lush. The other day I was seated at a bar with my pet duck under my arm, and this drunk came up to me and said. "Hey, you! Where did you get that pig?" I said, "This isn't a pig." And he said, "I WAS TALKING TO THE DUCK." Years of heartbreak and despair followed. But all things pass. One day I was walking in the lobby of my hotel and there he was again! Yes! You guessed. It was Brock talking to my old friend the Colonel. I laughed gaily. I didn't want them to see the cracks in my shattered heart. And I must have hidden my feelings pretty well. Because I overheard the Colonel say to Brock, "Is that Hortense?" And Brock replied, "SHE LOOKS PRETTY RELAXED TO ME." Brock said, "My darling, how wonderful to see you here in (LOCAL) after all these years. Tell me, what are you up to? And I said, "FIFTY DOLLARS." Then Brock gave a little moan. "O, Hortense," he said, "Can you ever forgive me for deserting you all those years ago?" And I told him a little poem that I had composed for just such an occasion:

THE MOON MAY KISS THE STARS ON HIGH;
THE BEE MAY KISS THE BUTTERFLY;
THE MORNING DEW MAY KISS THE GRASS,
AND YOU, DEAR BROCK, FAREWELL.

(*There is a chord from the ORCHESTRA. As HORTENSE
accepts her applause, the INTERLOCUTOR comes forward and joins her* C.)

INTERLOCUTOR. Ah, thank you, Countess. I'm sure we'll all
treasure your memories . . . at least until we leave the theatre.
And now, ladies, will you please join me in a tribute to the
greatest of all American instruments . . . the Banjo.

(*The PRIMA DONNA, the 1ST COMIC, and the SUGAR BA-
BIES begin a rousing minstrel walk-around. After a few
bars, the 1ST COMIC exits* R. *as the BANJO MAN [a member of the MALE ENSEMBLE] enters* L.)

"*MISTER BANJO MAN*"

(*ORCH: 2 Bar Intro*)

PRIMA DONNA & 1ST COMIC.
I LOVE THE SOUND OF A BANJO
LOVE THE JOY THAT IT BRINGS
I'VE BEEN A FAN OF THE MAN
PLUNKIN' ON THOSE STRINGS

PRIMA DONNA.
NOTHING MATCHES A BANJO
TO MAKE YOU KICK UP YOUR HEELS
OH WHAT A THRILL
I CAN'T STAND STILL
AND OH, HOW GOOD IT FEELS

(*BANJO MAN enters.*)

MISTER BANJO MAN
MISTER BANJO MAN
KEEP ON PLUNKIN' AWAY
LET THE MUSIC RING

WHILE WE DANCE AND SING
TILL THE BREAK OF DAY

MISTER BANJO BAN
MISTER BANJO MAN
YOU'RE THE GREATEST I SAY
EV'RY FINGER'S A REAL HUMDINGER
OH MISTER BANJO MAN
OH MISTER BANJO MAN
OH MISTER BANJO MAN PLAY

(*The PRIMA DONNA and the BANJO MAN dance for 32 bars.
Much of the dance is in the black light, which makes the
PERFORMERS seem to be energetic and enthusiastic
ghosts from minstrel shows of the past.* At the climax of
the duet, the lights return to normal.
The PRIMA DONNA accepts her applause, and both exit.
The SUGAR BABIES come forward, banjos in hand. Black
light again. The banjos glow with one color on the facing,
another on the back. The GIRLS use the different colors to
make patterns in the dark. The banjo ballet lasts for 26 bars.
Suddenly we see the garish dress of HORTENSE floating onto
the stage, and we know that the 1ST COMIC has returned.
So has the PRIMA DONNA. Normal light returns again,
and we are back to the vocal.*)

ALL.
MISTER BANJO MAN
YOU'RE THE MAN WHO CAN
CHASE MY WORRIES AWAY
WHILE YOU'RE STRUMMIN'
MY HEART IS HUMMIN'
OH MISTER BANJO MAN
MISTER BANJO MAN
MISTER BANJO MAN
PLAY

(*A final pose.*)

---

*NOTE: Black light was used on the variety stage as early as 1904, and in *The
Radium Girls of 1919* there were five such numbers.

THE CURTAIN FALLS

END OF ACT I

ACT TWO

Scene 1

CANDY BUTCHER

Who can forget the ubiquitous super-salesman of Burlesque, who peddled chocolates by promising us unspeakable delights — "books that will appeal to the most jaded reader of unusual fiction," "bonus gifts," "genuine postcards from France."

Alas, promise always exceeded performance, and, in that respect, the CANDY BUTCHER prepared us for the disappointments of life. Not that we learned from experience. In the Gaiety Theatres of our youth, we kept on buying his big combination offers on the slight chance that, maybe, just this one time, he was telling the truth.

In reality, these salesmen were not part of the performance proper, but franchised dealers who bought from the theatre the right to peddle their wares during the intermission.

Our CANDY BUTCHER, however, is a member of the CAST — one of the eccentric comedians who appears elsewhere in the show. Twelve minutes into the intermission, he enters down one of the aisles. He has a tray around his neck containing boxes of chocolates, magazines, and other articles. FOUR SALESMEN with identical trays enter with him. The advertising drop is down. After an 8-bar introduction from the ORCHESTRA, the CANDY BUTCHER addresses the audience in a loud and insinuating manner.

Candy Butcher. Ladies and Gentlemen, may I have your attention, please. You have approximately seven minutes before we continue our Big Burlesque Revue. You won't want to miss the first number in the Second Act, which is called "The Dance of the Virgins" — performed by our lovely ladies of the chorus strictly from memory. Now, to while away the time during this brief pause in the entertainment, you may feel the need for something to munch on. I have here a box of chewy, delicious chocolates. (*He holds up the candy.*) You buy these chocolates for the modest price of a quarter, and, not only do you get the chance at one of our special bonus gifts, but you also receive absolutely free all the items contained in our BIG COMBINA-

TION OFFER. Now, part one of our big combination offer is a spicy little booklet that you'll never find in the Salvation Army reading room. We're not permitted to sell this booklet, but nothing in the law says we can't give it away FREE as part one of our big combination offer. (*opens book*) Let me call your attention to page four of this little booklet. There you will find a story entitled "Love Below the Border." The author of this story calls a spade a spade. He pulls absolutely no punches. The hero of our story is a world traveller who meets a beautiful dance hall girl called Mexicali Rose. "Rose," he says, "I've seen beautiful girls before in Boston, New York, St. Louis, Cleveland and Chicago, but I never saw a girl quite so beautiful as you." They get better acquainted and she invites him back to her apartment. "Rose," he says, "I've seen beautiful apartments before, in Boston, New York, St. Louis, Cleveland and Chicago, but I never saw an apartment quite so beautiful as this one." She leaves the room to get into something more comfortable and comes back wearing a negligee. "Rose," he says, "I've seen negligees before in Boston, New York, St. Louis, Cleveland and Chicago, but I never saw a negligee quite so beautiful as this one." They begin to dance, and soon she invites him to come into her boudoir. "Rose," he says, "I've seen beautiful boudoirs before in Boston, New York, St. Louis, Cleveland and Chicago, but I never saw a boudoir quite so beautiful as this one." No sooner had they entered the boudoir than they began to make love. And when they began to make love, from then on, it was the same damn thing as Boston, New York, St. Louis, Cleveland and Chicago. What happens after that is nobody's business but your own. (*He puts the magazine in the tray and picks up a small novelty telescope.*) Part two of our big combination offer is this little novelty item imported from Paris, France. (*points to someone in the audience*) I see a doubter in our midst. Sir, if this little telescope doesn't come from Paris, France, may I drop dead on this spot. (*He steps to another spot. Then he holds the telescope up to his eye.*) You hold this little telescope up to the light and you will see a beautiful model wearing a two-piece outfit—spats. She wiggles and shakes. She shakes and wiggles. We call her Candy, because she'll make your peanut brittle. (*He puts a telescope in the tray and picks up a bottle of pills.*) Part three of our big combination offer is the big one—virility pills. These pills are truly a marital helper. But let me warn you, boys. When you take one of these pills, swallow it fast. Otherwise, you'll get a stiff neck. And don't take two of them. You'll pole vault out the window. Now, Ladies and Gentlemen, each of our young salesmen is working his way through reform school and would appreciate your patronage.

(*The SALESMEN pass through the audience, selling the chocolates and books. As they do, the CANDY BUTCHER keeps up a steady stream of talk. "Buy the chocolates for a quarter." "Get our big combination offer — the story about Mexicali Rose, the little novelty item imported from Paris, France." The SALESMEN echo his chatter. "Buy while the supply lasts," etc., etc.*)

CANDY BUTCHER. (*continuing, during the hubbub*) Hold up your prizes. Let us see them.

ONE OF THE SALESMEN. (*over the noise*) There's one of the bonus gifts. This gentleman has a watch.

CANDY BUTCHER. What kind of watch is it?

SALESMAN. A Gruen.

CANDY BUTCHER. A Gruen? That's the best Gruen you ever had, sir. (*The SALESMEN continue selling. Finally, the CANDY BUTCHER stops them.*) I see we have a skeptic in the audience. (*to someone in the audience*) This is not a fake, sir. And to prove it's not a fake, I'm going to pass out our big bonus prize — one hundred dollars — to anyone whose box of candy contains a yellow ticket.

MAN IN AUDIENCE. I have a yellow ticket.

CANDY BUTCHER. Then the hundred dollars is yours, sir, provided you can answer one simple question. What is the last thing your wife says to you before you go to sleep at night?

MAN IN AUDIENCE. That ain't hard.

CANDY BUTCHER. You win the hundred dollars. (*He exits. The SALESMEN exit up the aisle. The advertising drop is raised to reveal the pink traveller, and a brief OVERTURE ushers in the rest of the Second Act.*)

ACT TWO

SCENE 2

GIRLS AND GARTERS

Burlesque audiences were suspicious of novelty, and producers made every effort not to give them any. In the Gaiety The-

*atre, if not in life, one could count on the comfort of famil-
iar forms, the assurance that no expectation would be tricked.*

*Thus, no regular patron of Burlesque would be surprised to find
an "audience number" at the beginning of our Second Act. I
refer, of course, to a musical scene which allows the ladies
of the chorus some direct contact with the public.*

*"Audience numbers" were cut from a standard pattern and dif-
fered only in trim and accessories. On Broadway the trim
and accessories of "GIRLS AND GARTERS" were sump-
tuous. But a more modest version of the scene can also be
effective.*

Here, roughly, is the sequence of events:

The SOUBRETTE slips through the c. *opening in the pink
traveller. She is briefly clad, wears garters, and carries a
flashlight, or perhaps a mirror.*

*She sings a song of invitation during which she is quickly
joined by the entire complement of SUGAR BABIES, also
handsomely bedecked and begartered. They, too, have
flashlights.*

"I'M KEEPING MYSELF AVAILABLE FOR YOU"

(*ORCH: 4 Bar Intro*)

Soubrette.
HEAR THIS LULLABY
FROM A BABE IN ARMS
YOU'RE THE REASON WHY
I'VE BEEN SAVIN' ALL MY CHARMS

(*ORCH: 4 Bar Transition to Chorus*)

I'M KEEPIN' MYSELF AVAILABLE
FOR YOU
SO PAMPER ME, PLEASURE ME
SAY THAT YOU TREASURE ME, TOO
I'M KEEPIN' MYSELF AVAILABLE
FOR YOU
TELL ME THERE'S LOVE FOR ME
LUST FOR ME
SAVE YOURSELF JUST FOR ME, TOO

I'LL DO ANY LITTLE THING
DADDY ADORES
POWDER MY BACK
I'LL POWDER YOURS
TIT FOR TAT

I'M KEEPIN' MYSELF AVAILABLE
FOR YOU
SO CODDLE ME, CUDDLE ME
KINDLE MY FIRE
COMFORT ME, CRADLE ME
CLING WITH DESIRE
STICK TO MY TAIL
I'M AVAILABLE
ONLY FOR YOU

(*FEMALE ENSEMBLE enters.*)

ALL GIRLS.
I'M KEEPIN' MYSELF AVAILABLE
FOR YOU
SO DIAMOND ME, BANGLE ME
SPARKLE ME, SPANGLE ME TOO

I'M KEEPIN' MYSELF AVAILABLE
FOR YOU
SO HONEY ORCHID ME, POSY ME
COVER ME, COZY ME TOO

SHOW ME I'M THE ONE YOU NEED
SHOW ME A SIGN
YOU SHOW ME YOURS
I'LL SHOW YOU MINE
THIS FOR THAT

I'M KEEPIN' MYSELF AVAILABLE
FOR YOU
SO NUZZLE ME, NESTLE ME
NEXT TO YOUR HEART
NURTURE ME, NOURISH ME
NEVER DEPART

FOLLOW MY TRAIL
I'M AVAILABLE
ONLY FOR YOU

*(During the song, the GIRLS use their flashlights to tease and
flirt with the audience. Shortly before the song ends, there is
a BLACKOUT. For 8 bars, we are in darkness with only the
bobbing flashlights visible.
The music segues to:
ORCH: 4 Bar Transition as GIRLS get on Swings to song:*

"EXACTLY LIKE YOU"

*Lights up. At this moment in the Broadway version, the SOU-
BRETTE and SIX GIRLS are discovered in swings, soaring
over the footlights. The swings are pushed by SEVEN OTHER
GIRLS. Eventually the PUSHERS leave the SWINGERS to
their own devices, rush forward, and run into the audience.
The SOUBRETTE and COMPANY Onstage sing and flirt. The
GIRLS in the audience sit on appropriate laps, remove garters, and snap them in the direction of favored patrons.**
*Some substitute Onstage action can be found if the swings prove
impractical. For swings are not a sine qua non of the scene;
only the audience contact is)*

ALL GIRLS.
I KNOW WHY I'VE WAITED
KNOW WHY I'VE BEEN BLUE
PRAYED EACH NIGHT FOR SOMEONE
EXACTLY LIKE YOU

WHY SHOULD WE WASTE MONEY
ON A SHOW OR TWO
NO ONE DOES THOSE LOVE SCENES
EXACTLY LIKE YOU

---

*NOTE: Garter-snapping is a hoary tradition in Burlesque. It dates back, at least,
to Millie de Leon, "The Girl in Blue," a hot number of the circuits during the first
decade of this century. De Leon's generosity with her garters twice got her arrested.

SOUBRETTE.	GIRLS. (*background*)
YOU MAKE ME FEEL SO GRAND	FEEL SO GRAND
I WANNA HAND THE WORLD TO YOU	I'LL HAND YOU THE WORLD
YOU SEEM TO UNDERSTAND	OO-OO UNDERSTAND
EACH FOOLISH LITTLE SCHEME	OO-OO
I'M SCHEMING	OO-OO
DREAM	OO-OO
I'M DREAMING	OO-OO

ALL.
NOW I KNOW WHY MOTHER
TAUGHT ME TO BE TRUE
SHE MEANT ME FOR SOMEONE
EXACTLY LIKE YOU

(*ORCH: GIRLS swing while other GIRLS throw garters to
audience 8 Bars*)

NOW I KNOW WHY MOTHER
TAUGHT ME TO BE TRUE
SHE MEANT ME FOR SOMEONE
NOT A GLOOMY GLUM ONE
SOMEONE —
SOMEONE —
SOMEONE —
EXACTLY LIKE
— YOU

(*ORCH: Finish
The now garterless GIRLS finally rejoin their SISTERS. The
ascent to the stage is accompanied by much ad lib adjusting
of bras, and squeals of simulated embarrassment.
ONE GIRL perhaps flirts for an extra moment, arriving Onstage
only one breathless beat before the BLACKOUT.*)

ACT TWO

SCENE 3

THE COURT OF LAST RETORT

(*POLICEMAN discovered in one*)
POLICEMAN. Hear ye. Hear ye. The court of Common Pleas is now in session. Anyone with business before this court, make his presence known. No presents of less than twenty-five dollars accepted. All hail the Judge.

(*Traveller opens to reveal courtroom with High Judge's stand. STRAIGHT MAN [D.A.] is discovered.*)

D.A. All hail the Judge. All hail the Judge.
JUDGE. (*1ST COMIC pops up from behind bench.*) Who said, "To hell with the Judge?" Have we any juicy cases today?
D.A. We have a case of bigotry, Your Honor.
JUDGE. Bigotry? What's that?
D.A. A man is accused of marrying three wives.
JUDGE. That's trigonometry. (*reaches below bench, brings out an old-fashioned telephone receiver*) Excuse me, I have a phone call. Hello, this is Judge Yule . . . (*Phone rings late. JUDGE, D.A., and POLICEMAN look to the wings, as if to indicate that the Stage Manager has made an error. ALL pretend to be amused or disconcerted.*) You called? Oh, you're taking a public opinion survey. Do I think that judges should have to take an intelligence test? I'm afraid I don't understand the question. What's the first case?
D.A. We have a murder case.
JUDGE. It's about time! What's the case?
D.A. A woman did her husband in.
JUDGE. What's the woman's name?
D.A. Westfall.
JUDGE. Send in Mrs. Breastfall.
D.A. (*correcting him*) Westfall.
JUDGE. I'm going to have trouble with that name.

(*Enter PRIMA DONNA as MRS. WESTFALL, in a sexy black dress.*)

Mrs. Westfall. (*flirting with JUDGE*) Hello, Judgie.

Judge. Would you like to come over to my house and talk about the weather?

Mrs. Westfall. The weather?

Judge. Whether you will or whether you won't. (*He puts his leg over the Judge's bench and starts to ride it.*)

D.A. Judge, stand on your dignity.

Judge. It won't reach down that far. (*to MRS. WESTFALL*) Raise your right hand. Do you swear?

Mrs. Westfall. Constantly.

Judge. Be seated. (*She wiggles into her seat, accompanied by appropriate noises from the DRUMMER.*) Wind that up and set it for eight o'clock.

Policeman. (*who clearly finds MRS. WESTFALL an exciting woman*) May I be excused, Your Honor?

Judge. Yes, Phillips. Go down and pound your beat. (*POLICEMAN exits.*) Now, Mrs. Asphalt, tell the court exactly how it happened.

Mrs. Westfall. Well, Judgie, it was just like this. (*She crosses her legs. The JUDGE drops his mallet, disappears from view, reappears at stage level through a swinging door in the Judge's stand. He kneels down as if to pick up the mallet and, of course, stares at her legs.*)

D.A. What are you doing, Your Honor?

Judge. I'm taking a closer look at this case.

D.A. Oh, I see. Are you scrutinizing the defendant?

Judge. Not yet. But I may get lucky later on. (*He hits her knee. It moves reflexively.*)

D.A. Look, Your Honor. When you hit it, it goes up. (*JUDGE turns and appears to hit himself in the groin with the mallet. He turns around in pain as we hear the sound of birds twittering.*)

Judge. That's a beautiful diamond you're wearing.

Mrs. Westfall. Yes, it is, Your Honor. You've heard of the Hope Diamond?

Judge. Who hasn't heard of the Hope Diamond?

Mrs. Westfall. Well, this is the Westfall Diamond. It comes with a curse.

Judge. What's the curse?

Mrs. Westfall. Mr. Westfall.

Judge. What the hey. (*starts up to bench*) Now, tell this court exactly what happened on the night in question.

MRS. WESTFALL. Well, I was fast asleep in my boudoir at 3:00 A.M. when my husband burst in without touching the knocker.

JUDGE. Without touching the knocker? Must be a leg man.

MRS. WESTFALL. I was suspicious, Your Honor. I could tell by the look on his face that he was getting a little on the side.

JUDGE. What?

MRS. WESTFALL. He was getting a little on the side.

JUDGE. (*making a note to himself*) I didn't know they moved it. Go ahead.

MRS. WESTFALL. He wanted me to give him a hot, home-cooked supper.

JUDGE. Did you give it to him?

MRS. WESTFALL. Certainly not!

JUDGE. Well, I can't blame you. Who's gonna lay it on the table at three o'clock in the morning. I bet that made him mad.

MRS. WESTFALL. Oh, it did, Your Honor. He called me vile names. Then we began to wrestle. First I was on top. Then he was on top. Then I was on the bottom, and he was on top. Then he was on the bottom, and I was on top. Then we both wound up on top. (*Her gestures complement her words.*)

JUDGE. I never tried that position. What happened then, Mrs. Lockjaw?*

MRS. WESTFALL. He whipped out a gun.

JUDGE. (*mock outrage*) What?

MRS. WESTFALL. He whipped out a gun.

JUDGE. Was it a big one?

MRS. WESTFALL. Oh, about this big. (*Suggests with her hand gestures that the gun is very large, indeed.*)

JUDGE. He belongs in the book of records. What kind of gun was it?

MRS. WESTFALL. A repeater.

JUDGE. (*with a knowing look*) Ah! A repeater!

D.A. Yes, a repeater. You have a repeater, don't you, Judge?

JUDGE. No, all I've got is a little single shot . . . little puff of smoke comes out. What happened then, Mrs. Messhall?

MRS. WESTFALL. I grabbed his gun.

JUDGE. (*mock outrage*) What?

MRS. WESTFALL. I pulled on it, and we fought. I pulled on it,

---

*Or Fishballs, or Legcramp, or Fruitplate.

and we fought. I pulled on it, and we fought. And finally the gun went off.

JUDGE. Well, that was bound to happen. You pull on a gun long enough, it's gonna go off. (*to D.A.*) What have you got to say to all of this, Dudley?

D.A. Your Honor, ladies and gentlemen of the jury, there sits a woman who lies. She claims her husband came home at three o'clock in the morning in an intoxicated condition. The man worked hard all day. After work he stopped in for a drink—perhaps two or even three. But was he drunk? No, I say, Your Horseship, that man was . . .

JUDGE. (*after a short take*) Back it up. What did you call me?

D.A. I said, "Your Worship."

JUDGE. You sure there wasn't a little horse in there somewhere?

D.A. (*neighing*) Nay! Nay!

JUDGE. That sounds a little hoarse.

D.A. Well, when I woke up this morning I was a little hoarse. (*JUDGE bangs gavel.*) Who cares if it was three o'clock in the morning? He simply asked for something to eat. But did he get it? No! I say, Your Horseship.

JUDGE. That'll be enough horseship out of you. (*He bangs gavel.*)

D.A. That woman is guilty, and I demand that you give her the full extent of the law.

JUDGE. Who are you to demand?

D.A. I'm the District Attorney.

JUDGE. I'm Justice.

D.A. Justice who?

JUDGE. Just as good as you are. Now, Mrs. Basketball, tell us exactly where you shot your husband.

MRS. WESTFALL. (*pleased tone*) I shot him between the green beans and the asparagus.

D.A. There, you see, Your Honor, she's guilty. She admits it. She shot her husband between the green beans and the asparagus.

JUDGE. Well, it could have been worse.

D.A. How?

JUDGE. If she'd shot him two inches lower . . .

D.A. Yes?

JUDGE. She'd have caught him right in his zucchini.

MRS. WESTFALL. (*rising*) Your Honor! Your Honor! Are you going to give me a stiff sentence?

JUDGE. If I get a good night's sleep, you can depend on it. (*bangs gavel*) Now, I know the pain you're suffering, Mrs. Breakwind, but before I pass sentence, do you have anything to say in your own defense?

MRS. WESTFALL. Yes, Your Honor. I just want to say that my husband was a mean man. He used to beat me. (*JUDGE ad libs violent reactions throughout this speech.*) He used to chase me around the room, ripping off my clothes, using and abusing my body.

JUDGE. He should have been hung.

MRS. WESTFALL. Oh, he was.

BLACKOUT

ACT TWO

SCENE 4

IN A GREEK GARDEN

As the title suggests, this scene is what Burlesque producers called "a cultural number."

On Broadway it was a solo by the SOUBRETTE and was billed as a tribute to Rosita Royce, a famous Burlesque dancer who performed with trained doves.

Few choreographers will want to imitate the many-birded Broadway version of this scene, but here it is for the records:

The SOUBRETTE enters L. in front of a blue traveller. Draped in white robes like an antique statue, she sings a lush ballad.

"WARM AND WILLING"

(*ORCH: 4 Bar Orch Intro*)

SOUBRETTE.
LOVE IS FOR THE WARM AND WILLING
WAITING FOR THE WARM AND WILLING

LOVE IS OURS TO TAKE
OR TOSS ASIDE

TAKE THIS PROMISE TO YOUR HEART
AND LET YOUR LIPS REPEAT
KISSES ARE TOO SWEET
TO BE DENIED

SHOW ME THAT YOU'RE WARM AND WILLING
MAKE EACH GOLDEN MOMENT THRILLING
GIVE MY EMPTY ARMS
A WELCOME SIGN

WE CAN MAKE THE STARS GO SPINNING
AND THE EARTH STAND STILL
IF YOU'RE WARM AND WILLING
TO BE MINE

(*The traveller parts to reveal the Green Garden of the title—a
     moonlit drop painted in a naive, romantic style. The SOU-
     BRETTE steps onto a pedestal* c.
*As she strips pieces of her clothing, the DOVES fly from the
     wings, perch on her arms and breasts, and cover what she
     has just uncovered.*

ORCH: 16 Bar Instrumental for Birds)

IT WOULD BE
HEAVENLY
IF YOU'RE WARM AND WILLING
TO BE MINE
IF YOU'RE WARM AND
WILLING
TO BE
MINE

(*ORCH: Hold for 4 Bars*

*Played as described, the scene is amusing and effective. But the
     doveless producer need not despair. There are simpler ways
     of paying homage to the higher arts.*
Living pictures, for example, can be most effective.

Suppose that when the traveller parts, we see many FEMALE STATUES in our garden, arranged in form-revealing classical poses. Enter a FAUN or the GOD OF LOVE or a YOUTH [in any case, a MALE DANCER from the CHORUS.] He kisses the STATUES. They come to life. A ballet follows. At last the Gift of Life is withdrawn, and the STATUES resume their original pose.
Of such stuff are dreams made—at least in Burlesque shows)

ACT TWO

SCENE 5

OUR DIVINE DIVA

Chord. Enter STRAIGHT in tuxedo. He stands in front of the pink traveller.

STRAIGHT. And now, ladies and gentlemen, the management would like to introduce this week's feature attraction . . .

(*CANDY BUTCHER appears in the aisle with his tray around his neck. He has some balloons for sale.*)

CANDY BUTCHER. Rubber balloons, souvenirs, peanuts, candy, rubber balloons.

STRAIGHT. Wait a minute, Max. You can't sell your balloons here. There's a show going on.

CANDY BUTCHER. Gee, I'm sorry, Peter. You see I haven't been myself lately. I just got married and I haven't been getting any sleep.

STRAIGHT. Yeh, and that reminds me, Max. Don't forget to pull the shade down when you're in bed with your wife.

CANDY BUTCHER. What are you talking about!

STRAIGHT. I drove past your house last night. Your shade was up, and I saw you making love to your wife.

CANDY BUTCHER. Ha! The joke's on you. I wasn't home last night. (*HE does a delayed take then exits up the aisle shouting, "Rubber Balloons! Rubber Balloons."*)

STRAIGHT. Excuse the interruption. Ladies and gentlemen, this is the spot usually reserved for our featured dancer who, this week was to be queen of the shimmy, the fabulous Annie Mc-

Casser. But, through a booking error, little Annie was sent to the Cleveland Opera and the star intended for the Cleveland Opera, Madame Alla Gazaza, was given a two-week engagement here in our theatre. At first, Madame Gazaza was reluctant to appear in a Burlesque show, but I assured her that the Gaiety is no ordinary palace of vulgar entertainment and that our audiences know class when they see it. So let's give a typical Gaiety welcome to that Queen of the Mezzo Sopranos—Madame Alla Gazaza.

(Fanfare. STRAIGHT exits as curtain parts to reveal PRIMA DONNA as MADAME GAZAZA in evening gown against gold traveller. She is flanked by potted palms. S.L. is a piano. An ACCOMPANIST in tails plays an arpeggio. MME. GAZAZA begins singing an aria. Enter 1ST COMIC in the middle of the audience. He is dressed in overalls. He starts to hammer. She continues to sing for a few bars, then stops angrily.)

GAZAZA. What are you doing?

1ST COMIC. I'm hammering.

GAZAZA. But I'm singing.

1ST COMIC. Well, go ahead, sweetheart, you're not bothering me.

GAZAZA. What's the big idea?

1ST COMIC. Well, the manager told me to make some repairs. I'm fixing seats. (*to a lady in the audience*) Would you like to have your seat fixed?

GAZAZA. Now listen, little man. If you don't behave, I'm going to ask the manager to take you out.

1ST COMIC. I don't go out with managers.

GAZAZA. How dare you insult the great Gazaza! I have sung before the crowned heads of Europe.

1ST COMIC. (*removing hat to show bald spot*) And the bald heads of (*LOCAL*). (*1ST COMIC, in the audience, may find some occasions for ad lib comment here. If there is a bald man seated near him, HE might compare heads or make some appropriate comment like, "Pardon me, sir, I thought you were sitting upside down."*)

GAZAZA. What effrontery, young man! I have one of the most expensive voices in the world. I spent fifty thousand dollars to train this voice.

1st Comic. Fifty thousand dollars? You ought to meet my brother.

Gazaza. Is he a voice teacher?

1st Comic. No, he's a lawyer. He'll help you get your money back. (*He exits* l., *as she calls* o.r.)

Gazaza. Mr. Leeds. Mr. Leeds.*

Straight. (*enters* r.) What is it now, Madame Gazaza?

Gazaza. There's a little man out here, and he keeps insulting me.

Straight. What little man? (*apologetically*) Opera singers are very eccentric.

Gazaza. I am not eccentric.

Straight. Compose yourself, Madame Gazaza. The show must go on.

Gazaza. Yes, of course. Please excuse the interruptions, ladies and gentlemen. I will now try to sing a different tune. Maestro. (*She begins singing.*)

2nd Comic. (*enters* r. *with a mournful expression on his face*) Oh, why did he die? Why did he die?

Gazaza. (*stops singing*) Why did who die?

2nd Comic. My wife's first husband. Why did he die? (*Exits* l. *GAZAZA begins singing again.*)

1st Comic. (*enters* l.) Wait a minute! Wait a minute! Don't anybody move. I've lost it.

Gazaza. (*stops singing*) Lost what?

1st Comic. (*taking cord from his pocket*) Oh, there it is!

Gazaza. What?

1st Comic. The lost chord.

(*A blaring chord from the ORCHESTRA. 1ST COMIC makes a gesture of disapproval and exits* r. *Enter CHARACTER MAN* r., *looking into a large hand mirror.*)

Character. I can't believe it. It can't be. It can't be. It can't be. Who's that? (*He puts mirror up to GAZAZA's face.*)

Gazaza. Me.

Character. Thank God, I thought it was me. (*Exits* l. *GAZAZA is bewildered. She sings a note or two, but without much confidence. Enter 2ND COMIC,* l.)

---

*Substitute the real name of the STRAIGHT MAN.

2ND COMIC. Hey, how do you kiss the rear end of a duck without getting feathers in your mouth?

GAZAZA. I don't know.

2ND COMIC. (*pantomimes blowing, then kissing*) But you got to be fast. (*Exit* R. *GAZAZA sings briefly as JUVENILE enters* R., *skipping rope.*)

GAZAZA. What are you doing?

JUVENILE. I'm following doctor's orders.

GAZAZA. Doctor's orders?

JUVENILE. Yes, he told me to take some pills three days running, then skip a day. This is my day to skip. (*He skips* O.R. *GAZAZA seems about to sing, when 2ND COMIC enters* R., *with a mouthful of feathers.*)

2ND COMIC. (*to audience*) I wasn't fast enough. (*He exits* L. *as CHARACTER MAN enters* R.)

CHARACTER. (*trying to get her attention*) Madame. Madame. What's the difference between mashed potatoes and pea soup?

GAZAZA. I don't know.

CHARACTER. Anyone can mash potatoes. (*He exits* L. *as GAZAZA makes one last effort to sing. 1ST COMIC enters moaning.*)

1ST COMIC. Why did I do it? Why did I do it?

GAZAZA. Do what?

1ST COMIC. (*moaning*) I sold my wife for a bottle of whisky, and now I want her back.

GAZAZA. Do you miss her?

1ST COMIC. No, but I'm thirsty again. (*He remains on as SOUBRETTE enters* R. *She crosses the stage crying and bumping.*)

SOUBRETTE. My husband is dead, dead, dead. (*bump*) My husband is dead, dead, dead. (*Bump. She has reached 1ST COMIC.*) My husband is dead, dead, dead . . . DEAD! (*exits* L.)

1ST COMIC. (*calling off after her*) Honey, your husband ain't dead. He's hiding. (*He exits* R. *as CANDY BUTCHER appears in the* R. *aisle.*)

CANDY BUTCHER. Souvenirs. Candy. Rubber balloons. Get your rubber balloons.

GAZAZA. (*calling* O.R.) Mr. Leeds. Mr. Leeds.

STRAIGHT. (*entering* R.) What's the matter now?

GAZAZA. I'm nearing the end of my endurance. Why is that man selling balloons?

STRAIGHT. What's the matter with you, sir? I told you before you can't sell balloons while the show . . . By the way, do you sell refreshments, too?

CANDY BUTCHER. Sure.

STRAIGHT. Do you have popcorn balls?

CANDY BUTCHER. No, rheumatism makes me walk this way. (*He exits angrily up the aisle, hollering, "Rubber balloons."*)

STRAIGHT. (*very apologetically*) Continue singing, Madame Gazaza. You won't have any further trouble. (*He exits* R.)

GAZAZA. All right. Ladies and Gentlemen, I have a request. But I'm gonna sing anyway. I will now sing "One Fine Day" by Madame Butterfly. (*to ACCOMPANIST, sharply*) Hit it! (*She sings.*)

1ST COMIC. (*enters* L. *with a large light bulb*) Twenty years of my life I've devoted to this invention. My family has gone without food and shelter. But now I'll be rich; I'll be the toast of the scientific world. Finally it's perfected. The world will know me at last. (*talking into bulb as if it were a telephone*) Hello. Hello. (*1ST COMIC exits* R. *as JUVENILE and CHARACTER MAN enter* R., *running and quarreling.*)

JUVENILE. Take it back.

CHARACTER. I won't.

JUVENILE. You will.

CHARACTER. I won't. (*The JUVENILE shoots the CHARACTER MAN. The LATTER starts to fall. The JUVENILE runs quickly behind the CHARACTER MAN and catches him, dragging him* O.L.)

GAZAZA. (*almost hysterical*) Mr. Leeds, he's killed him! I can't stand it anymore!

(*STRAIGHT enters* R., *followed by a GORILLA on roller skates, carrying a bouquet.*)

STRAIGHT. Here's a fan of yours, Madame Gazaza. (*GORILLA skates toward her and presents her with the bouquet. GAZAZA doesn't see the BEAST until after she accepts the flowers.*)

GAZAZA. Oh, thank you . . . (*She sees the GORILLA, screams and faints. The STRAIGHT catches her, as the TWO COMICS enter, one from each side, to aid the STRAIGHT.*)

STRAIGHT. Rub her neck. (*TWO COMICS echo it.*) Rub her

arms. (*TWO COMICS echo it.*) Rub her shoulders. (*TWO COMICS echo it. Enter CANDY BUTCHER l. with balloons.*)
CANDY BUTCHER. Rubber balloons . . . rubber balloons . .

BLACKOUT

ACT TWO

SCENE 6

TROPICAL MADNESS

The best jokes are those in which the audience is persuaded, without rancor, to laugh at itself. The effect of such jokes depends on thwarted expectation. Witness the mock-strip-tease which forms the action of this brief scene.
In front of the pink traveller, the JUVENILE enters as PRO-DUCTION SINGER in white tie and tails. With him is a beautiful DANCER in evening dress, probably the SOU-BRETTE.
ORCH: 8 Bar Intro to Verse

"CUBAN LOVE SONG"

JUVENILE.
LIFE IS FILLED WITH GLORY
NOW THAT I KNOW OUR LOVE
WAS MEANT TO BE
EACH KISS TELLS THE STORY
WHILE MY HEART RINGS AND
SINGS OUR MELODY, DEAR

(*ORCH: 2 Bars into Chorus*)

I LOVE YOU
THAT'S WHAT MY HEART
IS SAYING
WHILE EV'RY BREEZE
IS PLAYING
OUR CUBAN LOVE SONG

I LOVE YOU
FOR ALL THE JOY
YOU BROUGHT ME
THE LOVELY NIGHT
YOU TAUGHT ME
OUR CUBAN LOVE SONG

ONE
MELODY WILL ALWAYS
THRILL MY HEART
ONE
KISS WILL CHEER ME
WHEN WE'RE
FAR APART
DEAR ONE

I LOVE YOU
WITH SUCH A TENDER PASSION
THAT ONLY YOU COULD FASHION
SUCH JOY AND ADMIRATION
AND SUCH A NEW ELATION
WITH RAPTURE AND DEVOTION
AND SUCH A GREAT EMOTION
THAT ALL THE WHILE I'M PRAYING

(*DANCER's bra comes off and reveals full-length gown.*)

I HEAR THE MUSIC PLAYING
OUR CUBAN
LOVE SONG

(*ORCH: 6 Bar exit music for JUVENILE and DANCER*

They begin what appears to be a straight vaudeville act—a ball-room dance specialty. He sings the verse of the song. As she twirls away from him, a piece of her dress comes off in his hands. He seems surprised. Encouraged by "the accident," she begins to remove other pieces of clothing. He continues singing and with increased excitement. She strips down to her black lingerie, as he approaches the climax of his song. She begins to remove her bra. When, after some apparent difficulty, she releases the catch, an evening dress falls from the bra and suddenly she is completely dressed. She exits triumphantly on the arm of the JUVENILE.)

BLACKOUT

ACT TWO

SCENE 7

CAUTIONARY TALES

(Three Blackouts)

(*In one. Traveller closed. No pause between these brief scenes.*)

a. *"Remedies"*

(*NURSE discovered next to a hospital screen, R. She is checking something on a clipboard. Enter 2ND COMIC from R. proscenium.*)

2ND COMIC. How do you do, nurse. I'd like to see the doctor.
NURSE. (*somewhat rudely*) Well, the doctor is very busy. You'll have to wait.

(*A scream of pain off stage. From behind the screen the 1ST PATIENT enters. His hand covers his left ear. He starts out toward R. proscenium.*)

2ND COMIC. Hey, bud, what's the matter with you?
1ST PATIENT. I have erysipelas [ear-i-sip-i-lus], so the doctor cut off my ear. (*He exits R. A second scream of pain from behind screen. Enter 2ND PATIENT, limping, with a bandage on his foot. He starts out R. 2ND COMIC stops him.*)
2ND COMIC. Hey, bud, what's the matter with you?
2ND PATIENT. (*pointing at his wounded foot*) I had ptomaine poisoning, so the doctor cut off my toe. (*He exits, limping.*)
2ND COMIC. Erysipelas, ear? Ptomaine poisoning, toe? (*starts to exit*) See you later, nurse.
NURSE. What's the matter with you?
2ND COMIC. I've got prickly heat.

CHORD. BLACKOUT

b. *"Poetic Justice"*

(*A table at a fancy restaurant [near* L. *proscenium]. Discovered at the table, an elegantly dressed WOMAN reading a menu. Beside her is a snobbish WAITER [the CHARACTER MAN] dressed in tails. He has a pencil and order pad.*)

WOMAN. How much is a nice filet mignon?

WAITER. Sixty-two cents.

WOMAN. Sixty-two cents? I'll take it. (*WAITER notes it on his pad.*) And how much is a bottle of your finest imported champagne?

WAITER. Twenty-three cents.

WOMAN. Twenty-three cents? How can you charge these ridiculously low prices?

WAITER. Very easily. Right now my boss is upstairs with my wife. What he's doing to her up there, I'm doing to him down here.

CHORD. BLACKOUT

c. *"Bait"*

(*2ND COMIC discovered* C., *fishing. He casts without success.*)

2ND COMIC. I've spent all day fishing on this pier and I haven't got a bite. Maybe I'm using the wrong bait. (*Enter* L., *1ST FISHERMAN. He has a pole and six fish on a string. 2ND COMIC stops him.*) Pardon me, bud. Did you catch all those fish on this pier?

1ST FISHERMAN. Sure did.

2ND COMIC. What did you use for bait?

1ST FISHERMAN. Well, I happen to be a doctor. This morning I performed a tonsillectomy, and I cut up the tonsils into little pieces and I used them for bait.

2ND COMIC. (*as 1ST FISHERMAN exits*) Thank you, Doctor. Well, I don't know where I'm going to get any tonsils. (*Enter* R., *2ND FISHERMAN, with rod and eight fish on a string. 2ND COMIC stops him.*) Hey, bud. Did you catch all those fish on this pier?

2ND FISHERMAN. Bet your life I did.

2ND COMIC. What did you use for bait?

2ND FISHERMAN. Well, you see, I happen to be a doctor, and this morning I performed an appendectomy. I cut up the appendix into little pieces and used that for bait. (*2ND FISHERMAN starts to exit.*)

2ND COMIC. Much obliged. (*to himself*) Tonsils, appendixes. Well, they're all catching fish. (*3RD FISHERMAN enters with more than a dozen fish on his string. As he crosses, 2ND COMIC stops him.*) Oh, pardon me, doctor . . .

3RD FISHERMAN. What doctor? I'm a rabbi.

CHORD. BLACKOUT

ACT TWO

SCENE 8

McHUGH MEDLEY

This medley is the "star turn," or what used to be called, in revues, the Eleven O'Clock Number, which, with today's early curtains, comes on at about ten-fifteen.
The 1ST COMIC and the PRIMA DONNA sing some songs by the principal composer of the show, Jimmy McHugh.

"McHUGH MEDLEY"

ORCH: 4 Bar Intro

1ST COMIC & PRIMA DONNA.
EV'RY WEEK ANOTHER TUNE
EV'RY WEEK ANOTHER TOWN
NEVER WANT TO LET THE ACT
GROW STALE

GET THE PROPS AND PACK THE TRUNK
THE SHOW GOES ON UNLESS YOU'RE DRUNK
KEEP IT FRESH
YOU CAN'T AFFORD TO FAIL

BUT WE HAVEN'T GOT A
REASON TO COMPLAIN
WE WERE BORN
TO SING AND ENTERTAIN

(*ORCH: Ad Lib Transition*

1ST COMIC goes to piano and plays elaborate introduction.)

    PRIMA DONNA. Sing!
    1ST COMIC.
I CAN'T GIVE YOU ANYTHING
BUT LOVE, BABY
THAT'S THE ONLY THING
I'VE PLENTY OF, BABY

DREAM AWHILE, SCHEME AWHILE
YOU'RE SURE TO FIND
HAPPINESS AND, I GUESS
ALL THOSE THINGS
YOU'VE ALWAYS PINED FOR

(*ORCH: Orchestral accompaniment with 1ST COMIC's piano now begins.*)

GEE, I'D LIKE TO SEE YOU
LOOKING SWELL, BABY
DIAMOND BRACELETS
WOOLWORTH DOESN'T SELL, BABY
TILL THAT LUCKY DAY
YOU KNOW DARN WELL, BABY

(*ORCH: Orchestral accompaniment stops, 1ST COMIC finishes alone.*)

I CAN'T GIVE YOU ANYTHING
BUT LOVE

(*ORCH: 4 Bar Intro to "I'M SHOOTIN' HIGH"*)

    PRIMA DONNA.
I'M SHOOTIN' HIGH
GOT MY EYE
ON A STAR
IN THE SKY
SHOOTIN' HIGH

I'LL NEVER STOP
TIL I GET
TO THE TOP
TELL ME WHY
SHOULDN'T I

YOU KNOW IT'S YOU I'M AFTER
YOU'RE MY LUCKY STAR
I'M ON A RAINBOW RAFTER
CLIMBING UP TO WHERE YOU ARE

I'LL HAVE A TIME
IT'S A CLIMB
BUT I'LL MAKE IT CAUSE
I'M
SHOOTIN' HIGH

CLIMBING UP
TO THE TOP
I AM NOT
GONNA STOP
CAUSE I'M
SHOOTIN' HIGH

(*ORCH: 2 Bar Finish*

ORCH: Ad Lib Intro during 1ST COMIC's costume change)
   1ST COMIC. (*spoken with a Scottish brogue*) Och . . . It's a broadlich, moonlicht nicht tonicht. Ah, lads and lassies, it's great to be lookin' into your faces . . . and believe me, some of your faces need lookin' into. (*He now sings, Ad Lib*)

I WANDERED TODAY
TO THE HILL
MAGGIE
TO WATCH
THE SCENE BELOW

   PRIMA DONNA. I don't believe what I'm hearing!
   1ST COMIC.
THE CREEK AND THE
CREAKING OLD MILL

MAGGIE
AS WE USED TO
LONG, LONG AGO

(*ORCH: Vamp begins under dialogue.*)

1ST COMIC. How do you like it, Annie?
PRIMA DONNA. Oh, Mick, that was terrible.
1ST COMIC. Well, didn't you see the gleam in me eye?
PRIMA DONNA. Ah, 'tisn't the gleam in your eye.
1ST COMIC. Well, what is it?
PRIMA DONNA. 'Tis the tilt of your kilt!
1ST COMIC. What the hey! Can ya fix it?
PRIMA DONNA. Well, I can try . . . Professor! (*She sings.*)

YOU SIMPLY
TAKE A FAVORITE
THEN YOU FLAVOR IT
WITH A NOTE OR TWO

OF BLUE HARMONY
TELL THE ORCHESTRA TO
PLAY STACCATO
AND THEN YOU
JAZZ A LITTLE OBLIGATO

NOW THAT MAGGIE TUNE
IS A RAGGIE TUNE
PAY NO ATTENTION
TO THE MUSIC THAT
THEY PLAY BUT
JUST ROCK
YOUR BLUES
AWAY

(*ORCH: Vamp begins under dialogue.*)

1ST COMIC. I like it! I like it!
PRIMA DONNA. You're a man of taste and distinction!

(*ORCH: 1 Bar Intro*)

Prima Donna.   1st Comic.
YOU SIMPLY   I
TAKE A FAVORITE   WANDERED TO-
THEN YOU FLAVOR IT   DAY TO THE
WITH JUST A NOTE OR   HILL
TWO OF
BLUE HARMONY   MAGGIE, TO
TELL THE ORCHESTRA   WATCH THE
TO
PLAY STACCATO   SCENE BE-
AND THEN YOU JAZZ   LO - O -
A LITTLE OBLIGA-   O - W
TO

NOW THAT MAGGIE   THE CREEK AND THE
TUNE
IS A RAGGIE TUNE   CREAKING OLD
PAY NO ATTENTION TO   MILL
THE
MUSIC THAT THEY   MAGGIE
PLAY BUT
JUST ROCK   AS WE USED TO LONG
YOUR BLUES AWAY   LONG A - GO - O
ON THE SPOT   O - O - O
START TO SWAY   O - O - O
GETTIN' HOT
NOW

HEAR THE BROKEN   THE GREEN GROVE IS
TIME
JUST SPOKE IN TIME   GONE FROM THE
ALL AROUND I SEE   HILL
HARMONY, CHARMIN'   MAGGIE, WHERE
ME
EV'RY LOVIN' NOTE   ONCE THE

IS A LOVIN' BOAT   DAISIES
JUST FULL OF MUSIC   SP - R -
THAT YOU CAN'T RE-   UNG
FUSE   BUT I
NOW YOU KNOW THE   LOVE YOU THE
WAY

TELL THE BAND TO　　　SAME AS IN
PLAY
AND WHEN YOU LISTEN　OLD
JUST
CHRISTEN IT AND SAY　 MAGGIE
I'VE
GOT THOSE　　　　　　 WHEN
WHEN YOU AND I WERE　YOU AND
YOUNG MAGGIE　　　　 I WERE
BLUE – OO – OO'S　　　 YOU – NG

　　BOTH.
IT'S VERY
EASY ONCE YOU
GET THE HANG
TO TAKE AN
OLD-TIME DITTY
DADDY SANG
AND MAKE IT
NICE AND RAGGIE
LIKE THE
EVER LOVIN'
MAGGIE
BLUES

(*They both speak in tempo.*)

The
Ever lovin'
Maggie
Blues
Yeah!

(*ORCH: Rideout Ending and Segue to Vamp leading to "SUNNY
　　SIDE OF THE STREET"*

1ST COMIC tries on hat.)

　　PRIMA DONNA. Wrong! (*1ST COMIC tries on another hat.*)
Wrong!! (*1ST COMIC tries on hat for a third time.*) Wrong!!!
　1ST COMIC. Well, what do you want me to put on?

(*ORCH: Tempo into Song*)

PRIMA DONNA.
GRAB YOUR COAT
AND GET YOUR HAT
LEAVE YOUR WORRIES
ON THE DOORSTEP
JUST DIRECT YOUR FEET
TO THE SUNNY SIDE OF THE STREET

CAN'T YOU HEAR THAT PITTER-PAT
AND THAT HAPPY TUNE
IN YOUR STEP
LIFE CAN BE SO SWEET
ON THE SUNNY SIDE OF THE STREET

I USED TO WALK IN THE SHADE

1ST COMIC. (*answers*)
SHE USED TO WALK IN THE SHADE
PRIMA DONNA.
WITH MY BLUES ON PARADE
1ST COMIC. (*answers*)
WITH HER BLUES ON PARADE
PRIMA DONNA.
BUT I'M NOT AFRAID
1ST COMIC. (*answers*)
SHE'S NOT AFRAID
BOTH.
THIS ROVER
CROSSED OVER

AND IF I NEVER HAVE A CENT
I'LL BE RICH AS ROCKEFELLER
GOLD DUST AT MY FEET
PRIMA DONNA.
ON THE SUNNY SIDE
1ST COMIC.
SHE SAID THE FUNNY SIDE
BOTH.
THE PEACHES
CREAM AND
THE HONEY SIDE
CROSS ON OVER TO
THE SUNNY SIDE OF THE
— STREET

(ORCH: Rideout Ending, 4 Bars

*Although originally conceived as a two-handed scene, the med-
    ley can be performed by three or four PRINCIPALS, if the
    situation warrants. Any variety talents possessed by the per-
    formers should be displayed in this number. If one of the
    PRINCIPALS plays the piano, let her accompany the others
    for one song. If there is a soft-shoe DANCER in the crowd,
    let him shuffle into his specialty.
Needless to say, the arrangement of the final song permits a
    spectacular applause-catching exit at the* R. *proscenium,
    after which the PRINCIPALS return for their bows.)*

BLACKOUT

ACT TWO

Scene 9*

OUR FIRST ANNUAL SHIMMY CONTEST

*Chord. STRAIGHT and JUVENILE enter in front of pink
    traveller. JUVENILE has an easel which he places near* L.
    *proscenium. Numbered cards are stacked on the easel with a
    blank card on top.*

Straight. (*to ORCHESTRA LEADER*) Glen, if you
please . . .

*(Fanfare. Traveller parts to reveal four to six GIRLS posed in
    front of a blue drop. The GIRLS wear costumes heavily em-
    bellished with shimmering fringe.)*

---

*NOTE TO PRODUCERS: In the Broadway production, the McHugh medley
was followed by a vaudeville act (Bob Williams' sketch about a dog-trainer
whose spaniel refuses to perform). Burlesque shows of this period often featured
one or two legitimate variety turns. The producer may wish to be guided by the
Broadway example and use an animal act or other specialty number in this next-
to-closing position. Or he may wish to present this shimmy contest, which requires no special arrangement of music—only an ad lib drum accompaniment
for the dancers.

Straight. (*continued*) Ladies and Gentlemen, Monday [or whatever day] is Chorus Girl Opportunity Night at the Gaiety Theatre. Some of our delightful Sugar Babies will compete for your applause, the winner to receive a year's contract in the theatres of the Mutual Burlesque Association. You are the judges, Ladies and Gentlemen, so reserve your most enthusiastic approval for the girl of your choice. So, here it is, the first annual shimmy contest of the Gaiety Theatre. (*The 1ST GIRL comes Forward and the JUVENILE holds a card saying #1 over her head. Drum roll. As the 1ST GIRL shimmies, she sings a simple scale. While she is performing, the STRAIGHT keeps up a running commentary.*) The first of our Sugar Babies, Miss Mitzi Malone, possesses a lyric soprano voice of magnificent compass and clarity, having been educated for Grand Opera. While performing her shimmy, Miss Malone will scale the heights. (*The audience, encouraged by the JUVENILE, applauds. This ritual isrepeated with four or five more GIRLS.*) The second of our Sugar Babies, Miss April May, was educated at a convent school in Spain, then abducted by gypsies, who taught her the quaint and curious native dances of their remote region. Here she is, Ladies and Gentlemen, playing with her Iberian castinets. (*During this speech, MISS MAY does a combination Spanish dance and shimmy. JUVENILE holds a #2 card over her head. Applause.*) Our third Sugar Baby is our première danseuse, Miss Donna Van. Miss Van studied with the nephew of Nijinski, practised her pirouettes at the Paris Opera and brings to the mysteries of the shimmy a rare sense of classical dignity and style. (*A shimmy on pointe here. Same business for STRAIGHT and JUVENILE.*) Our fourth dancer, Miss Joanne Smart, ran away from school at the age of nine to join an Italian circus. Unfortunately the circus soon disbanded, but Miss Smart, displaying the ready aptitude for which our girls are famous, had already absorbed many of the secrets of the tanbark. As a tumbler she has achieved the rank of International Grand-Master, Second-Class, and tonight promises all of you a head-over-heels performance. (*an acrobatic shimmy*) Our fifth Sugar Baby is Miss Anna Strogoff, a bronze medalist in gymnastics at last year's Pan-Hungarian Tournament of Champions. Tonight her ample accomplishments are yours to contemplate, Ladies and Gentlemen, as she brings to her shimmy the grace and suppleness of a trained professional in her demanding field. Miss Anna Strogoff. (*an athletic shimmy with runs and splits*)

And now, I pray silence, Ladies and Gentlemen; our next dancer, Miss Libby Roulade, the daredevil of the Sugar Babies, will perform a feat of great dancer and difficulty. She will shimmy blindfolded, Ladies and Gentlemen, and this hazardous undertaking requires great concentration. Reserve your thunderous applause for the conclusion of her performance. Miss Libby Roulade. (*During this speech, and with appropriate percussion backing, MISS ROULADE has been led forward by the JUVENILE. She is very uninhibited in her shimmy.*) Our seventh Sugar Baby, Miss Marianne Nicole, is the daughter of a general in the French Foreign Legion. She brings to her shimmy the sense of military precision which she learned while on maneuvers behind her father's parade ground. Here is our saucy sergeant-major, Miss Marianne Nicole.

(*A military tap dance shimmy. Note: one can have as many or as few contestants as the situation seems to call for. All or some of the above can be used; or others can be written to suit the special talents of the chorus. In any case the scene ends as follows:*)

STRAIGHT. (*continued*) Our next Sugar Baby, Miss Norma Caprice, has promised us an exhibition of great originality and daring. Despite our prodding, she has refused to reveal even to us the novel features of her performance. Here is that lady of mystery, Miss Norma Caprice. (*MISS NORMA CAPRICE has a wild look in her eye, and although stripping is forbidden, she is sufficiently imbued with the spirit of competition to rip off her bra near the climax of her dance, making sure, of course, that thereafter she faces demurely* us. *Her daring awakens the spirit of emulation among her fellow CONTESTANTS, and soon chaos reigns, while the STRAIGHT MAN and JUVENILE in mock rage and horror rush about as if they were desperate to restore order. The JUVENILE covers offending bosoms with his number cards, and the STRAIGHT MAN pulls several GIRLS* us. *as he calls for the asbestos to be dropped. The asbestos is dropped; the STRAIGHT MAN silences the ORCHESTRA and wipes his brow with what he thinks is his handkerchief. It is, in fact, a discarded bra which he has picked up in the confusion. HE is embarrassed and puts it behind his back.*) I must apologize, Ladies and Gentlemen. There is no question that Girl No. 6 exceeded the bounds of decency and good taste. You will be happy to learn that she has been disqualified from the contest, and her applause will be redistributed equally among the other contestants. You have been so generous in your appreciation of the other girls that we have decided to continue this contest through the remaining performances of this engagement. Cumulative applause totals will be kept, and the winner will be announced on the evening of January 18, 1908. And here, Ladies and Gentlemen . . . (*The asbestos has been raised to reveal the blue traveller.*) . . . is the entire company, supported by Madame Hilda and the Red Raven Cadets in a tribute to that Grand Old Man, who is the father of us all. (*Traveller parts and in to the FINALE.*)

ACT TWO

SCENE 10

OLD GLORY

Our archetypal Burlesque show comes to its archetypal conclusion with that most popular ritual of the variety stage — a grand patriotic finale.

Such finales come in all shapes and sizes, and, if he wishes, the choreographer may depart from the sequences recorded here — provided, of course, that he pays tribute to the appropriate national symbols and conjures up an exuberant, colorful display.

Lights up on a pink traveller. Enter CHARACTER MAN. He is wearing tie and tails, but in a bright color, not black.

CHARACTER. (*as ANNOUNCER*)* And now, Ladies and Gentlemen, here is the entire company — supported by Madame Hilda and the Red Raven Cadets — in a tribute to that grand old man, who is the uncle of us all.

(*The blue curtains part to reveal [in front of the gold traveller] the male PRINCIPALS, dressed, like the CHARACTER MAN, in brightly-colored formal suits. Enter 1ST COMIC, in a slightly more elaborate version of the same costume,*

---

*If the shimmy contest is not used.

with an admiral's hat and a ribbon that says, "Ambassador of Good Will."

ORCH: 2 Bars Intro)

GAIETY QUARTET.
ARE YOU FEELING LOW
BUS'NESS KINDA SLOW
HAVE YOU PAID YOUR
INCOME TAXES YET

DON'T IT MAKE YOU BOIL
WHEN YOU THINK OF OIL
AND THE TANKERS
THAT THIS COUNTRY
DIDN'T GET

WE'RE TANGLED UP IN
FOREIGN TROUBLES
AND IT SEEMS A SHAME
SO TELL US
WHO'S TO BLAME

1ST COMIC. (*Solo*)
YOU CAN'T BLAME
YOUR UNCLE SAMMY
FOR HE'S BEEN MIGHTY
GOOD TO YOU

HE CAN'T HELP CONDITIONS
IF CROOKED POLITICIANS
DO WHAT THEY DO
TO OUR RED, WHITE
AND BLUE

GAIETY QUARTET.
WE'VE ALWAYS BEEN THE GOATS
'CAUSE WE GO AND GIVE OUR VOTES
TO THE MEN WHO PICK OUR POCKETS
WITH A GRIN
1ST COMIC. (*solo*)
BUT YOU CAN'T BLAME

YOUR UNCLE SAM — MY
IT'S THE COMPANY
THAT HE'S BEEN
IN

*(ORCH: 2 Bar Intro to 20 Bar George M. Cohan Dance Section
    with 1ST COMIC and MALE and FEMALE DANCERS.*
*The first part of the song is staged as a dialogue between the 1ST
    COMIC and the OTHER MEN. They tell us about current
    problems in America [ca. 1925], and he replies that "You
    can't blame your Uncle Sammy; It's the company that he's
    been in."*
*The gold traveller then parts to reveal a drop of New York har-
    bor on which the Statue of Liberty is prominently painted.
    A gaily-decorated platform is a few feet DS. of the drop,
    and, between the two, we see some ship models [a cutter, a
    destroyer, etc.], as if bobbing on the waves.*
*Discovered also are four male and eight female DANCERS in
    red-white-and-blue sailor suits. A 20-bar dance sequence
    follows, performed by the 1ST COMIC and the ENSEM-
    BLE in imitation of the style of George M. Cohan.*
*The DANCERS exit as six SHOWGIRLS enter. To our surprise
    we discover that the aforementioned ship models are, in
    fact, headdresses for the GIRLS, who also are wearing wide
    paniers of flag material, cut away to reveal shapely legs in
    flesh-colored tights.)*

    1ST COMIC. (*reciting as the GIRLS enter*)
AND NOW A SPECIAL TRIBUTE
TO THE SHIPS WHAT SAIL THE SEAS
TO SYMBOLIZE THE NAVY
MEET THE FRIGATES IF YOU PLEASE

(ORCH: 2 Bar "Bump and Grind" Section

*The SHOWGIRLS bump, grind, and turn US. Their costumes
    are backless. There is only one concession to modesty; on
    each beautiful behind is a skimpy, but carefully placed, an-
    chor of blue cloth.*
*The SHOWGIRLS mount the platform as the 1ST COMIC exits
    L., and the PRIMA DONNA enters R. in a cut-away se-
    quined military uniform. She sings a verse and chorus of*

*the song, supported by the ENSEMBLE. Then, without accompaniment except for the taps of her own shoes, she puts the DANCERS THROUGH a military drill.**

ORCH: 6 Bar Intro to PRIMA DONNA section)

PRIMA DONNA.
IF YOU TAKE A LOOK
IN YOUR HIST'RY BOOK
YOU WILL FIND THAT
WHAT I SAY IS TRUE

PARTY POLITICS
NEVER SEEM TO MIX
WITH THE LOVE THAT
UNCLE SAMMY HAS FOR YOU

IF THE MEN THAT YOU'VE ELECTED
DOUBLECROSS YOU, THEN I CLAIM
YOU HAVE YOURSELF
TO BLAME
PRIMA DONNA & ENSEMBLE.
YOU CAN'T BLAME
YOUR UNCLE SAMMY
FOR HE'S BEEN MIGHTY
GOOD TO
YOU
PRIMA DONNA. (*solo*)
HE'S HAD LOTS OF PATIENCE
WITH ALL THOSE FOREIGN NATIONS
THEY OWE A DEBT
THAT THEY SEEM TO FORGET

PRIMA DONNA.	ENSEMBLE. (*background*)
IT KIND OF MAKES YOU SORE	OO — OO
THEY KEEP ASKIN' US FOR MORE	OO — OO

---

*This section of the finale commemorates a famous act — Madame Hilda and the Red Raven Cadets — who were headliners on the Empire Circuit in 1905. As the climax of their act, the Cadets "scaled a wall in the military fashion."

AND THE WAY THEY   OO — OO
TAKE ADVANTAGE   OO — OO
IS A SIN
   ALL.
BUT YOU CAN'T BLAME
YOUR UNCLE SAM - MY
IT'S THE COMPANY
THAT HE'S BEEN
IN
   PRIMA DONNA. Company . . . Attention!!

(ORCH: PRIMA DONNA Military Tap Dance Section begins

*This drill can be as simple or as complex as the time and talent
   permit: a plain march, for example, or a series of compli-
   cated maneuvers, including gun tucks and a live volley. At
   the end of the drill, the MALE DANCERS lift the PRIMA
   DONNA and carry her O.R.*

ORCH: 4 Bars)

   PRIMA DONNA.
HUP HUP HUP HUP HUP
HUP HUP HUP HUP

(ORCH: 4 Bars)

   PRIMA DONNA.
AND 1

*(ORCH: 4 Bars
       8 Bars
       4 Bars
       6 Bars
ORCH: 2 Bars Music Reenters as PRIMA DONNA executes
   a series of turns around the stage. 10 Bars)*

   ENSEMBLE.
UNCLE!
(ORCH: 2 Bars)
SAMMY!
(ORCH: 2 Bars)
UNCLE!

(*ORCH: 1 Bar*)
SAMMY!
(*ORCH: 1 Bar then 4 Bar Finish to PRIMA DONNA lift.*
ORCH: 20 Bar Tap Dance with ENSEMBLE.
*The DANCERS begin an enthusiastic 20-bar tap dance sequence.
Then the 1ST COMIC returns as do the rest of the MALE
PRINCIPALS. ALL sing a final verse and chorus. The drop
of the harbor disappears and is replaced by a giant Ameri-
can flag.*
ORCH: Build to Return of Vocal
*The PRIMA DONNA now re-enters as the STATUE OF LIB-
ERTY. She is held aloft by the MALE DANCERS over the
heads of the rest of the COMPANY. Add sparklers, bal-
loons and/or confetti to taste.*)

ENTIRE COMPANY.
YOU CAN'T BLAME
YOUR UNCLE SAMMY
FOR HE'S BEEN MIGHTY
GOOD TO YOU

IF YOU ARE DISGUSTED
WITH ONE OR TWO HE'S TRUSTED
THINK OF THE REST
WHO ARE DOING THEIR BEST
1ST COMIC. (*solo*)
THIS LAND THAT GAVE US BIRTH
IS THE GREATEST ONE ON EARTH
IF THINGS GO WRONG
JUST WEAR IT WITH A GRIN
ENTIRE COMPANY.
CAUSE YOU CAN'T BLAME
YOUR UNCLE SAMMY
IT'S THE COMPANY
THAT
HE'S
BEEN
IN

(*ORCH: 12 Bar Coda*)

THE CURTAIN FALLS

PROPERTIES LIST:

ACT ONE

I,i OPENING

Stethoscope	Nurse (Sugar Baby #3)
Large Hypodermic Needle	Nurse (Sugar Baby #3)
Billy Club	Gaiety Quartet #4
Cigar	Juvenile
Purse with Compact &	
Hankie on String	Sugar Baby #1
Two Large White Balloons	Sugar Babies #7 & #8
Hedge with Scissors on top	Gaiety Quartet #1
Two Large Wooden Hoops	Sugar Babies #7 & #8
Hankie	Sugar Baby #2
Two Seltzers	Sugar Babies #5 & #6
Flit Can	Sugar Baby #12

I, ii NO PROPS

I, iii NO PROPS

I, iv

Four Purses (One Breakaway,	
One Weighted)	See Costume List

I, v

Fourteen Green Suitcases	Sugar Babies #1 - #14
Five Train Cars	Sugar Babies #1 - #14
Engine with Carbon Dioxide	Sugar Babies #1 - #14
Caboose	Sugar Babies #1 - #14
Luggage Cart	Prima Donna & Gaiety
	Quartet #1 - #4

I, vi

One Old Leather Suitcase	Second Comic
Hotel Desk with:	
Two Stick Telephones	

Hotel Bill
Potted Palm
  Bell
Money (bills)   First Comic

I, vii NO PROPS

I, viii

Knifeboard with Silhouette of
    man painted on it
Small Table with Knives
Money   Prima Donna
Cigarette   Prima Donna

I, ix NO PROPS

I, x

a) NO PROPS
b) Money - Two Bills   Second Comic, Second
                                    Character
c) Mortgage   Straight
    Money   Soubrette
d) Rocking Chair
    Newspaper   Second Character
e) Notepad & Pen   Straight

I, xi

Piano on Wheels

I, xii NO PROPS

I, xiii

Teacher's Desk
Two Rolled Newspapers
Four Student's Desks with
    Chairs
One Bentwood Chair
One Blackboard

Pointer   Prima Donna
Bell   Prima Donna

I, xiv NO PROPS

I, xv

Fourteen (14) Bentwood
  Chairs
Fifteen (15) Banjos   Sugar Babies #1 - #14 &
                                  Gaiety Quartet #3
One Banjo Stool   Gaiety Quartet #3
Fourteen (14) Tambourines
One Throne/Armchair   Prima Donna

ACT TWO

II, i

Five Candy Butcher Trays   Eccentric Comedian &
                                  Gaiety Quartet #1 - #4
Box of Candy   Eccentric Comedian
Packets of SUGAR BABIES
  Candies   Gaiety Quartet #1 - #4
Booklet/Magazine   Eccentric Comedian
Small Novelty Telescope   Eccentric Comedian
Bottle of Pills   Eccentric Comedian

II, ii

Fifteen (15) Flashlights   Soubrette and Sugar
                                  Babies #1 - #14
Garters   All Sugar Babies Not on
                                  Swings

II, iii

Courtroom Bench
Small Desk & Chair
Witness Chair
Gavel
Two American Flags
Stick Telephone

II, iv NO PROPS

II, v

Candy Butcher Tray	Eccentric Comedian
Rubber Balloons on Sticks	Eccentric Comedian
Potted Palm	
Small Table	
Hammer and Bang Board	First Comic
One Sash Cord	First Comic
Large Light Bulb	First Comic
Starter's Pistol w/6 Blanks	Offstage
Upright Piano	
Feathers	Second Comic
Mirror	First Character
Jump Rope	Juvenile
Gun	
Roses for Gorilla	Sugar Baby #1

II, vi NO PROPS

II, vii

a)

One Stethoscope	Nurse (Sugar Baby #3)
One Ear Bandage	Gaiety Quartet #3
One Foot Bandage	Gaiety Quartet #1
Clipboard (Pad & Pencil)	Nurse (Sugar Baby #3)
Doctor's Office Screen	

b)

Restaurant Table	
Menu	Sugar Baby #10
Waiter's Cloth	Second Character
Writing Pad	Second Character
Pencil	Second Character
One Bentwood Chair	Sugar Baby #10

c)

One Pole With Six Fish on	First Comic
One Fishing Pole	Second Comic
Two Poles With Fish	Straight & Eccentric Comic

II, viii

Grand Piano
Piano Stool

II, ix

Easel (With Numbered
   Cards)   Juvenile

II, x

Statue of Liberty Torch
   (Lites)   Prima Donna
Statue of Liberty Tablet   Prima Donna
Four American Flags in
   Holders   Sugar Babies #7 - #10
Eight Guns   Sugar Babies #7 - #14

ACT ONE

1. A Memory of Burlesque (Opening)
FIRST COMIC—red long underwear, baggy pants, overcoat, battered top hat, white dickey with tie, tennis shoes
JUVENILE—black tailsuit with white vest, white tux shirt, white bowtie, white gloves, black shoes
SOUBRETTE—black and white dress, hat and purse, fur piece, white gloves, black shoes
1ST CHARACTER—black pants, white shirt, black bow tie, striped jacket, apron, black shoes
GAIETY QUARTET #1—checked shirt, brown overalls, work gloves, straw hat, black shoes
GAIETY QUARTET #2—black pants, black sweater, black gloves, black hat with mask, black shoes
GAIETY QUARTET #3—night shirt, robe, slippers, head bandage
GAIETY QUARTET #4—2-piece policeman uniform and hat, black shoes, white gloves
SUGAR BABY #1—pink and orange tootsie dress, pink shoes, orange hat
SUGAR BABY #2—antique lace dress with orange slip, orange and black velvet coat with fur collar, long black gloves, black head band with feather, black shoes

SUGAR BABY #3 — padded nurse dress, nurse cap, white shoes
SUGAR BABY #4 — pink panties, butterfly wings with drapes, antennae, toe shoes, snap-on butterflies
SUGAR BABIES #5 & #6 — short red firecoats, fireman hats, black shoes
SUGAR BABIES #7 & #8 — two-piece acrobat leotards, green choker and wristbands, ribbon headpieces, aqua jazz oxfords
SUGAR BABIES #9 & #10 — body stockings, mesh unitard with silver balls, silver ball hat, ballet slippers
SUGAR BABY #11 — pink bellydancer skirt, pink bra with coins, pink veil with coins, gold shoes
SUGAR BABY #12 — exterminator jumpsuit, lightweight duster, pith helmet with netting, black shoes
SUGAR BABIES #13 & #14 — short white ambulance jackets with Red Cross emblems, white shorts, white pillbox hats with Red Cross emblems, white shoes

2. *Welcome to the Gaiety*

STRAIGHT — three-piece black tuxedo, white tux shirt, black bow tie, black shoes
2ND CHARACTER — blue suit, striped shirt, tie, black shoes

3. *Every Girl A Star ("Let Me Be Your Sugar Baby")*

GIRLS CHORUS (SUGAR BABIES #1-#14) — blue and pink Sugar Babies Costume, beaded net tights, pink boots, blue hat with pink feathers

4. *Meet Me Round The Corner*

JUVENILE — three-piece black and white plaid suit with carnation and pocket watch, white shirt, tie, black shoes
2ND COMIC — maroon baggy pants, checked 3/4 length comic coat, tan vest, striped shirt, short tie, hat, long black shoes
STRAIGHT — blue two-piece suit, shirt, tie, black shoes
1ST COMIC — red underwear, morning coat, striped morning pants, dickey with tie, tennis shoes
1ST GIRL (SUGAR BABY #3) — orange and yellow fringed hooker dress, orange hat, fur piece, orange gloves, purse, necklace, black shoes
2ND GIRL (SUGAR BABY #1) — blue, green and yellow hooker dress, feather boa, necklace, purse, green hat and gloves, black shoes
3RD GIRL (SUGAR BABY #2) — turquoise pleated hooker dress,

ostrich boa, black hat and gloves, purse, bracelet, black shoes

SOUBRETTE — fuschia and lavender hooker dress, lavender gloves, lavender shoes, lavender hat, purse

5. Travelin'

GIRLS CHORUS (SUGAR BABIES #1–#14) — blue lace nightie, lace underpants, hair bows, aqua tap shoes with lavender bows

BOYS CHORUS (GAIETY QUARTET) — three-piece green conductor suit, conductor's hat, collarless shirts, collars, black tap shoes, black ties

PRIMA DONNA — two-piece royal blue travelling suit, black feather boa, black gloves, black stockings, gold tap shoes

6. Broken Arms Hotel

CLERK (2ND CHARACTER) — three-piece pinstripe suit, blue shirt, red tie, black shoes

BELLBOY (1ST CHARACTER) — bellboy jacket, pillbox hat, black pants, white gloves, black shoes

FIRST COMIC — red underwear, morning pants with suspenders, tennis shoes

OLD MAN (2ND COMIC) — three-piece morning tuxedo, tux shirt, tie, spats, black shoes, white gloves

YOUNG BRIDE (SUGAR BABY #3) — ecru 1930's wedding dress, veil, ecru shoes

7. Feathered Fantasy (Sally Rand)

JUVENILE — black tailsuit with white vest, white bow tie, white gloves, black shoes, tux shirt

GIRLS CHORUS (INCLUDING SOUBRETTE OR FEATURED SUGAR BABY, PLUS 11 OTHER GIRLS) — sequined body stocking, gold shoes, two aqua ostrich feather fans

8. World's Greatest Knife-Thrower

ANNOUNCER (STRAIGHT) — three-piece black tuxedo, white tux shirt, black bow tie, black shoes

KNIFE-THROWER (PRIMA DONNA) — multicolored full skirt, white gypsy blouse, leather vest, black boots, gypsy scarf and hat, earrings, bracelets and chains, wide belt, whip

FIRST COMIC — sport shirt, slacks, sneakers

9. Ellis Island Love Story ("Immigration Rose")

FIRST COMIC—two-piece blue suit with rose, blue cap, pink-striped shirt, tie, black shoes

GAIETY QUARTET (ALL FOUR)—various plaid or checked pants and bests, collars, collarless colored or striped shirts, bow ties, black shoes

10. Scenes from Domestic Life

a) Burglar

2ND COMIC—grey checked jacket, taupe baggy pants, red cap, blue checked vest, blue striped shirt, short tie, long black shoes

SOUBRETTE—long black robe with ostrich trim, black shoes

b) Betting

2ND CHARACTER—blue two-piece suit and accessories (see I, ii)

2ND COMIC—same as in previous scene

c) Philadelphia

VILLAIN (STRAIGHT)—blue-striped suit with matching vest, striped shirt

FATHER (1ST CHARACTER)—black pants, white collarless shirt, black shoes, blue sweater

NELL (SOUBRETTE)—blue gingham dress with white apron, black stockings, black shoes

d. Dutiful Daughters

FATHER (2ND CHARACTER)—same as in previous scene (I, x, b)

1ST DAUGHTER (SUGAR BABY #11)—blue and white check dress, black shoes

2ND DAUGHTER (SUGAR BABY #7)—green and white checked dress, black shoes

3RD DAUGHTER (SUGAR BABY #6)—brown and white checked dress, black shoes

e. Monkey Business

POLICEMAN (STRAIGHT)—blue pants, white shirt, black shoes, policeman's hat

SOUBRETTE—policeman's coat, black shoes

11. Torch Song ("Don't Blame Me")

PRIMA DONNA—black one-sleeved sequined dress, black feather headpiece, black shoes, jewelry

ACCOMPANIST (GAIETY QUARTET #3)—top hat, checked pants, "Ed Wynn" overcoat with fur lapels, vest shirt, glasses, black shoes

12. Orientale
ANNOUNCER (2ND CHARACTER) — same blue two-piece suit (see above)
BELLY DANCER (SUGAR BABY #1) — purple shaded belly dance skirt, beaded bra, jeweled headpiece, veil, silver shoes

13. The Little Red Schoolhouse
TEACHER (PRIMA DONNA) — blue long skirt with petticoat, white blouse with black bow, black shoes
1ST GIRL (SUGAR BABY #11) — green and white lace dress, green tights, hairbow, black flat shoes
2ND GIRL (SUGAR BABY #3) — pink and white lace dress, hairbows, pink tights, white flat shoes
2ND COMIC — blue knickers, sailor shirt, blue striped socks, straw hat, long black shoes
FIRST COMIC — red underwear, brown shirt with large Peter Pan collar, plaid shorts with suspenders, straw hat, wig, short boots

14. Presenting the Springboard Sisters ("Sugar Baby Bounce")
SOUBRETTE — hot pink beaded bra, pink beaded and pleated chiffon skirt, beaded necklace and wristbands, pink beaded head band with feather, silver shoes
SISTER #1 (SUGAR BABY #1) — identical outfit in turquoise
SISTER #2 (SUGAR BABY #7) — identical outfit in lavender

15. Madame Rentz and her All-Female Minstrels
ANNOUNCER (2ND CHARACTER) — same as previous scene (I,x,b)
GIRLS CHORUS (ALL
  SUGAR BABIES) — striped leggings, red tailcoat with pleated bib and collar, white gloves, red tophats, orange spats, black shoes
PRIMA DONNA (INTERLOCUTOR) — white leotard, white tailcoat with jeweled lapels, jeweled bow tie, white gloves, white jeweled tophat, white spats, white tap shoes
FIRST COMIC — drag dress (glows in the dark), glitter tennis shoes, black leg garter, hair bows
BANJO MAN (GAIETY QUARTET #3) — orange pants with mesh dickey, white blouse, white gloves with black trim, orange and pink vest, white spats, orange hat, black shoes

ACT TWO

1. Candy Butcher
ECCENTRIC COMEDIAN / CANDY BUTCHER—blue pants, blue
   shirt, tie, white jacket, black shoes
SALESMEN (GAIETY QUARTET #1-4)—white jackets, checked,
   striped or plaid pants, shirts, black shoes

2. Girls & Garters
SOUBRETTE—white costume with purple maribou balls, lavender
   garter belt, lavender stockings, lavender shoes, white hat
   with maribou balls
GIRLS CHORUS (SUGAR BABIES #1-#14)—pink costumes with
   maribou, purple garter belts, purple stockings, neckbands
   and armbands, four-strap gold shoes, black tri-corner hats
   with maribou balls

3. The Court of Last Retort
POLICEMAN (1ST CHARACTER)—policeman uniform, policeman
   hat, black shoes
D.A. (STRAIGHT)—two-piece blue double-breasted suit, blue
   tie, brown striped shirt, black shoes
JUDGE (1ST COMIC)—judge's robe, coveralls, tennis shoes,
   judge's wig
MRS. WESTFALL (PRIMA DONNA)—black dress with handkerchief
   hem, black picture hat with rose, black shoes and stockings,
   jewelry (must include diamond ring), black purse

4. In A Greek Garden ("Warm & Willing")
SOUBRETTE—body stocking, mesh jeweled unitard with sand
   drapes, jeweled necklace and perches at the bust and crotch,
   gold shoes, gold Grecian hat

5. Our Divine Diva (Madame Alla Gazaza)
STRAIGHT—black three-piece tuxedo, tux shirt, black bow tie,
   black shoes
CANDY BUTCHER—same as in previous scene (II, i)
GAZAZA (PRIMA DONNA)—black lace and purple diva dress,
   jewelry, black shoes
ACCOMPANIST (GAIETY QUARTET #1)—black tailsuit with white
   vest, grey spats, tux shirt, black shoes
FIRST COMIC—overalls, t-shirt, cap, tennis shoes

2ND COMIC—baggy gold pants, grey checked jacket, brown vest, striped shirt, derby hat, short tie, black long shoes

CHARACTER (1ST)—maroon plaid jacket, maroon baggy pants, shirt, tie, porkpie hat, black shoes

JUVENILE #1 (GAIETY QUARTET #3)—brown two-piece double breasted suit, shirt, tie, black shoes

SOUBRETTE—black dress, black pillbox hat with veil, black shoes

JUVENILE #2 (GAIETY QUARTET #2)—checked knickers, shirt, sweater, cap, socks, black shoes

GORILLA (SUGAR BABY #1)—gorilla costume, roller skates

6. Tropical Madness ("Cuban Love Song")

JUVENILE—tuxedo with black vest, black bow tie, tux shirt, black shoes

DANCER (SOUBRETTE OR SUGAR BABY #2)—seven-piece pull-apart dress, black panties, black bra, black Austrian drape, jewelry

7. Cautionary Tales

a) Remedies

NURSE (SUGAR BABY #3)—padded nurse dress, nurse cap, white shoes

2ND COMIC—large patchwork pants, checked jacket, striped shirt, knitted wool cap, short tie, long black shoes

1ST PATIENT (GAIETY QUARTET #3)—brown two-piece double breasted suit, shirt, tie, black shoes

2ND PATIENT (GAIETY QUARTET #1)—checked pants, striped collarless shirt, collar, bow tie, black shoes

b) Poetic Justice

WOMAN (SUGAR BABY #10)—turquoise leotard, turquoise skirt, hat with veil, black shoes, jewelry

WAITER (2ND CHARACTER)—black tailsuit, tux shirt, bow tie, black shoes

c) Bait

2ND COMIC—same as in previous scene (II, vii, a)

1ST FISHERMAN (STRAIGHT)—blue windbreaker, blue pants, shirt, hat, black shoes

2ND FISHERMAN (1ST CHARACTER)—blue sweater, black pants, white shirt, fishing cap, creel (pouch)

3RD FISHERMAN (ECCENTRIC)—blue pants, white shirt, tie, yellow windbreaker, fishing hat

8. *McHugh Medley*

FIRST COMIC—three-piece grey striped suit, blue-striped shirt, black shoes, various hats, kilt

PRIMA DONNA—blue and black leotard with ascot, black split skirt, black sequined jacket, various hats, black shoes

9. *Shimmy Contest*

STRAIGHT—black tuxedo, white tux shirt, black bowtie, black shoes

JUVENILE—black tuxedo, white tux shirt, black bowtie, black shoes

MITZI (SUGAR BABY #4)—royal blue velvet bra with fringe, blue velvet pleated skirt with fringe, silver shoes

APRIL (SUGAR BABY #5)—red and black ruffled bra with fringe, red and black ruffled skirt, mantilla and castinets, black shoes

DONNA (SUGAR BABY #6)—pink satin bra with fringe, short pink tulle skirt, toe shoes

JOANNE (SUGAR BABY #7)—blue, green and yellow harlequin unitard with fringe, harlequin hat, black ballet slippers

ANNA (SUGAR BABY #8)—orange velvet bra with fringe, orange pleated skirt with fringe, gold shoes

LIBBY (SUGAR BABY #9)—lavender bra with fringe, lavender pleated skirt with fringe, silver shoes

MARIANNE (SUGAR BABY #11)—khaki shorts, khaki bra with fringe, French Legionnaire hat, tap shoes

NORMA (SUGAR BABY #12)—body stocking, yellow bra with fringe, yellow pleated skirt with fringe, black shoes

10. *Old Glory*

GAIETY QUARTET—dark blue pants with red stripe, blue military jackets with white belts, military hats, black tap shoes

FIRST COMIC—two-piece blue double-breasted suit, "Ambassador of Good Will" banner, white shirt, red, white and blue tie, bi-corner hat with feather trim, black shoes

PRINCIPAL MEN (1ST & 2ND CHARACTERS, 2ND COMIC, STRAIGHT, ECCENTRIC, JUVENILE)—blue three-piece tailsuit with white vest, red and blue banner, white tux shirt, white bowtie, black shoes

TAP GIRLS (SUGAR BABIES #7–14)—dark blue shorts with gold fringe, red, white and blue sailor jackets, sailor hats, blue gloves (3/4 length), red tights, gold tap shoes

Soubrette—light blue and white pannier with anchor at rear, boat hat, gold shoes
Boat Girls (Sugar Babies #1-6)—red, white and blue panniers with anchors at rear, boat hats, gold shoes
Prima Donna—red sequined jacket with blue banner, red sequined hat, tap shoes

Bows
Soubrette—red fringed dress
Prima Donna—gold sequined dress, Statue of Liberty gold hat, gold shoes
(for bow, add red feather boa)

Other Publications for Your Interest

LITTLE SHOP OF HORRORS
(ALL GROUPS—MUSICAL COMEDY)

Book and Lyrics by HOWARD ASHMAN
Music by ALAN MENKEN

5 men, 4 women—Combination Interior/Exterior

Based on the film of the same name by Roger Corman. Screenplay by Charles Griffith. Look Out, here comes Audrey II! Live, and in Living Color, thrill to the excitement as Seymour, lowly assistant to florist Mr. Mushnik, desperately tries to satisfy the voracious craving for human flesh of the unearthly plant which seems to grow before our very eyes, singing and dancing its way into our hearts—literally. Sigh as Seymour tries to win the love of Audrey I (also known as Audrey), who also works in the shop. Her sado-masochistic dentist (isn't that redundant?) boyfriend becomes quite a tasty meal for the plant: but not its last! Suspense! Laughter! Chills! Music! Drama! And, a "60's Girl-Group" Chorus! "Adorable little spoof."—W.W. Daily. "Gleefully gruesome. This horticultural horror will have you screaming with laughter."—N.Y. Post. "It leaves the audience feeling just like Audrey II between victims—ravenous for more."—N.Y. Times. This long-running off-Broadway success was originally produced by the excellent W.P.A. Theatre in NYC.

(#666)

A DAY IN HOLLYWOOD/
A NIGHT IN THE UKRAINE
(ADVANCED GROUPS—MUSICAL REVUE)

Book and Lyrics by DICK VOSBURGH
Music by FRANK LAZARUS
Additional Music and Lyrics by Various Composers

4 men, 4 women, 1 pianist on stage, 2 pianists backstage—2 Sets

"Hollywood" is a marvelous nostalgic spoof of Hollywood and the movies of the 1930s that will delight both those who remember it and those too young to have known it. "Ukraine" is the comedy the Marx Brothers didn't make, but could have. It is ever-new, ever-fresh Marx Brothers updated and transformed into comic symbols of their time. This is a "musical double feature" and like the old movie double-header there is no connection between the two acts. But together it is fascinatingly successful. "The puns have wings . . . you leave the theatre with the dizzy feeling of having witnessed a super, impossibly professional senior-class spring show. Not a bed feeling, at all."—N.Y. Daily News. "It is crazy, zany magic . . . a smashing show, classy, sassy nostalgia."—N.Y. Post. "Act One is a splendidly funny and remarkably clever entertainment, Act Two has inspired lunacy, impeccable foolishness and perfectly hilarious nonsense."—WCBS-TV2. "A real winner . . . consists of two extended sketches, both gems."—Wall Street Journal.

A Day in Hollywood/A Night in The Ukraine (#6658)
A Night in The Ukraine (#16057)

Other Publications for Your Interest

A . . . MY NAME IS ALICE
(LITTLE THEATRE—REVUE)
Conceived by JOAN MICKLIN SILVER and JULIANNE BOYD

5 women—Bare stage with set pieces

This terrific new show definitely rates an "A"—in fact, an "A-*plus*"! Originally produced by the Women's Project at the American Place Theatre in New York City, "Alice" settled down for a long run at the Village Gate, off Broadway. When you hear the songs, and read the sketches, you'll know why. The music runs the gamut from blues to torch to rock to wistful easy listening. There are hilarious songs, such as "Honeypot" (about a Black blues singer who can only sing about sex euphemistically) and heartbreakingly beautiful numbers such as "I Sure Like the Boys". A . . . *My Name is Alice* is a feminist revue in the best sense. It could charm even the most die-hard male chauvinist. "Delightful . . . the music and lyrics are so sophisticated that they can carry the weight of one-act plays".—NY Times. "Bright, party-time, pick-me-up stuff . . . Bouncy music, witty patter, and a bundle of laughs".—NY Post.   (#3647)

I'M GETTING MY ACT TOGETHER AND TAKING IT ON THE ROAD
(ALL GROUPS—MUSICAL)
Book and Lyrics by GRETCHEN CRYER
Music by NANCY FORD

6 men, 4 women—Bare stage

This new musical by the authors of *The Last Sweet Days of Isaac* was a hit at Joseph Papp's Public Theatre and transferred to the Circle-in-the-Square theatre in New York for a successful off-Broadway run. It is about a 40-year-old song writer who wants to make a come-back. The central conflict is between the song writer and her manager. She wants to include feminist material in her act—he wants her to go back to the syrupy-sweet, non-controversial formula which was once successful. "Clearly the most imaginative and melodic score heard in New York all season."—Soho Weekly News. "Brash, funny, very agreeable in its brash and funny way, and moreover, it touches a special emotional chord for our times."—N.Y. Post.   (#11025)

ON THE TWENTIETH CENTURY

(ALL GROUPS—MUSICAL COMEDY)

Book and Lyrics by ADOLPH GREEN and BETTY COMDEN, Music by CY COLEMAN

17 principal roles, plus singers and extras (doubling possible)—Various sets

Whether performed with elaborate scenery, or on a simple skeletal scale, this brilliantly comic musical can appeal to audiences everywhere. This is truly an extravagant show—but its extravagance lies not in its scenery and physical production, but in the boisterous, tumultuous energy—and in the lush and sprightly energetic surge of its very melodic score. The story concerns the efforts of a flamboyant theatrical impressario to persuade a film star to appear in his next production, to outwit rival producers and creditors, to rid himself of religious nut Letitia Primrose (played by Imogene Coca on Broadway) and Lily's film star boyfriend Bruce Granit (who's as strong in profile as he is weak in brains). And, he must do all this before the famed 20th Century Ltd. reaches NYC! The story, and it's two leading characters—the mad impressario Oscar Jaffe and the love of his life and his greatest star Lily Garland—can be loved and enjoyed by all audiences. "Spectacular . . . funny . . . elegant . . . civilized wit and wild humor."—N.Y. Times. "A perfect musical . . . a gorgeous show! "—N.Y. Post.　　　　　　　(#819)

KURT VONNEGUT'S GOD BLESS YOU, MR. ROSEWATER

(MUSICAL SATIRE)

By the creators of LITTLE SHOP OF HORRORS

Book and Lyrics by HOWARD ASHMAN
Music by ALAN MENKEN
Additional lyrics by DENNIS GREEN

10 men, 4 women (principals—also double smaller roles),
extras, musicians—Various interiors and exteriors

"One of Vonnegut's most affecting and likeable novels becomes an affecting and likable theatrical experience, with more inventiveness, cockeyed characters, high-muzzle-velocity dialogue and just plain energy that you get from the majority of playwrights."—Newsweek. Eliot Rosewater's a well-intentioned idealist and philanthropic nut—and as president of a multi-million family foundation dispenses money to arcane and artsy-crafty projects. He's also a World War II veteran with a guilt complex, haunted by all this wealth—and also slightly crazy. His outlandish behavior enrages his senator dad, alienates his society-conscious wife—and the money attracts a young, shyster lawyer who tries to divert it to an obscure branch of the family. It portrays Vonnegut's vision of money, avarice and human behavior—as it aims a satrical fusillade at plastic America, fast foods, trademarks, slogans, media blitzes and the follies of materialism. "A charming, delightful, unexpected and thoughtful musical."—N.Y. Post.　　　　　　　(#630)